ESL Pathways: Bri

English for Intermediate Level Language Learners

MW00892025

By:

Daniel Harrington
Kimberly Heeren
David Treanor

Bridges

Intermediate

Bridges is an intermediate level language-learning textbook for adult learners.

Features of this book include:

● 48 Content-based conversation topics

● A wide variety of interesting subject matter

● Emphasis on comprehension and discussion

● Ideal for both individual and group instruction

Table of Contents

Lesson 1 — American Federal Holidays

- Do you celebrate Christmas? What do you do?
- When is New Year's Day? How is it celebrated?
- What is your favorite holiday?
- How many days off do you have in one year?
- What do you like to do on your days off?
- Do you think you have enough holidays?
- What American holidays do you know about?

Read about some American federal holidays.

American holidays are spread throughout the year. There are holidays and important dates in almost every month. A holiday is a day of remembrance for a person or an event. On some holidays you may have a day off from work but not on all of them. Having a day off and taking a vacation always mean that you do not have to go to work or school but a holiday, in the American sense, is generally a special day with historical significance.

The following is a list of federal holidays. The government recognizes these days as official days of significance. Work schedules may or may not be affected by these holidays. In the United States, there are 10 federal holidays set by law. The following four holidays are set by date.

New Year's Day	**January 1st**
Independence Day	**July 4th**
Veterans Day	**November 11th**
Christmas Day	**December 25th**

If any of the above falls on a Saturday, then Friday may be observed as a holiday. Similarly, if one falls on a Sunday, then Monday may be observed as a holiday.

The other six federal holidays are set by a day of the week and month.

Martin Luther King's Birthday	**Third Monday in January**
Washington's Birthday	**Third Monday in February**
Memorial Day	**Last Monday in May**
Labor Day	**First Monday in September**
Columbus Day	**Second Monday in October**
Thanksgiving	**Fourth Thursday in November**

Comprehension Questions:

1. What is a holiday?
2. Is a holiday a day off from work?
3. How is a holiday different from a vacation?
4. How many holidays does law in the United States set?
5. How many holidays are set by date?
6. How many are set by day of the week and month?
7. When is Independence Day?
8. What holiday is on November 11th?
9. What holiday is on December 25th?
10. What happens if a holiday falls on a Saturday?
11. What holiday is the third Monday in February?
12. When is Martin Luther King's birthday?
13. When is Washington's Birthday celebrated?
14. What holiday is the second Monday in October?
15. When is Thanksgiving?
16. When is Labor Day?
17. When is Memorial Day?
18. Which is first: Columbus Day or Martin Luther King's birthday?

Discussion Questions:

1. What are some important holidays in your country?
2. What is your favorite holiday? Why?
3. What special things do you do on different holidays?
4. What special things do you eat or drink on different holidays?

5. If you have a day off from work or school, what do you usually do?
6. Would you rather have time off on a rainy day or a sunny day? Why?
7. How many hours do you work or study in one week?
8. Do you feel that you have enough free time? Why or why not?
9. Would you rather go to work or stay home? Why?

10. Do you think people work too much? Why or why not?
11. Do you think there are enough holidays in your country? Why?
12. If the government decided to make a new holiday, what would be your suggestion? What would be the name of your holiday? What would be the date?

13. How long is a normal working day in your country?
14. What is the difference between full-time and part-time jobs?
15. Why do some people have two jobs?
16. Would you like to have two jobs? Why?
17. Have you ever had a part-time job? If so, what was it? Why did you decide to get this job? Did you enjoy the work? Why?

18. Do you think men should work more than women? Why?
19. Should men and women get equal pay? Why?
20. Can men and women do the same kinds of jobs? Why?

Superstitions

- Are you superstitious? Why or why not?
- What is the difference between superstition and science?
- Do you believe in witches?
- Do you believe in ghosts?
- Have you ever seen a ghost?
- Do you usually have good luck or bad luck?

Read about some common Western superstitions.

These are some common Western superstitions. Many of them originated during a time when there were no scientific explanations for events that happened. People used to believe in witches, magic, dragons, and fairies. There are still people who continue to believe in superstitions and live their lives according to these beliefs.

Superstition	Meaning
Baseball Bat	Spit on a new bat when using it for the first time to make it lucky.
Bed	It's bad luck to put a hat on a bed.
Bell	When a bell rings, an angel has received its wings.
Cats	If a black cat crosses your path, you will have bad luck.
Clover	It's good luck to find a four-leaf clover.
Knives	If a friend gives you a knife, you should give him/her a coin.
Ladybugs	It is bad luck to kill a ladybug.
Ladder	It's bad luck to walk under a ladder.
Mirror	If you break a mirror, it's seven years bad luck.
Salt	If you spill salt you must throw some over your left shoulder.
Umbrella	It's bad luck to open an umbrella in the house.
Wood	Knock on wood anytime you mention good fortune.
Yawn	Cover your mouth so your soul doesn't go out of your body.
Itchy Ear	Someone is talking about you.
Friday the 13th	This day is traditionally unlucky unless you were born on it.

Comprehension Questions:

1. What should you do to a bat to make it lucky?
2. What shouldn't you put on a bed?
3. How can cats be unlucky?
4. What kind of clover is good luck?
5. If a friend gives you a knife, what should you give in return?
6. How can ladders be unlucky?
7. How can ladybugs be unlucky?
8. What can give you seven years bad luck?
9. If you spill salt, what should you do?
10. How can umbrellas be unlucky?
11. When should you knock on wood?
12. What should you do when you yawn?
13. What does an itchy ear mean?
14. How can Friday the 13th be lucky?

Discussion Questions:

1. How do you feel about superstitions? Why? Are you superstitious?
2. Are you religious? Do you believe in a god?
3. What is your family's religion? What religious things do you and your family do?
4. Why do you think people continue to believe in superstitions?
5. Do you know anyone who is very superstitious?
6. Do you know anyone who is very religious?
7. Have you ever met anyone who has seen a ghost? Where did they see it?

8. What numbers are lucky in your country? Why?
9. What numbers are unlucky in your country? Why?
10. Do you have a lucky number? What number? Why is this your lucky number?
11. What lucky things have happened to you recently?
12. What unlucky things have happened to you recently?
13. In some western countries a rabbit's foot or a horseshoe is considered to be a lucky charm. What things are considered to be lucky charms in your country?
14. Do you carry a lucky charm? What do you do if you want to have good luck?

15. Make a list of some common superstitions in your country. Try to explain where they came from and why people believe in them. Include lucky and unlucky things.

Superstition	Reason

Lesson 3   Who's the Best Person for the Job?

- What do secretaries do? Make a list.
- What skills should a secretary have?
- Is being a secretary a good job? Why?
- Are secretaries usually male or female?
- Are bosses usually male or female? Why?
- What do trade companies do?

Read the following situation.

Trade Winds is an international trade company based in Hong Kong. They import goods from Mainland China and export to Europe, Australia and the USA. Mainly they deal with clothing and accessories. In the future they would like to expand their markets. They would like to do business with Mexico and some other countries in South America. The president of Trade Winds believes it is important for businesses to find new markets and to increase their sales. This way they can increase profit, and their employees can get higher salaries and better benefits.

Right now Trade Winds Company needs to hire a secretary for the marketing division. Twenty people have applied for the job and the personnel department has chosen four final applicants out of the original twenty. There are two males and two females. Two are from Hong Kong and the other two are from Mainland China and The UK. They each have good skills, high level of education and are all qualified for the job. The company needs to consider the applications of these final four applicants. Then they need to make a decision about which person is most suitable for the job. There are many things to consider when hiring a new employee.

Read about the four applicants:

Name:	Susan Tsai	Martin Lee	Peggy Wang	Robert Peel
Nationality:	Hong Kong	Hong Kong	China	United Kingdom
Education:	B.A. English	B. A. Finance	B.A. Math and Business	B.A. Secretarial studies
Age:	30	34	28	24
Typing speed:	60 WPM	55 WPM	60 WPM	65 WPM
Languages:	Cantonese, Mandarin, English	Cantonese, English, Spanish	Mandarin, English	English, Spanish
Experience:	8 years as a secretary	7 years in international trade sales	4 years as a secretary	None. Just graduated
Personality:	Serious, organized	Outgoing, funny	A little shy, quiet	Enthusiastic, a little gullible

Comprehension Questions:

1. What kind of company is Trade Winds?
2. Where is the company based?
3. What do they import? What do they export?
4. What do they mainly deal with?
5. What do they want to do in the future?
6. Where would they like to do business?
7. What does the president of Trade Winds believe?
8. Who do they need to hire?
9. What are the final four applicants' names?
10. Where are they from?
11. What kind of education do they have?
12. How old are they?
13. What are their typing speeds?
14. What languages can they speak?
15. How much experience does each have?
16. Describe their individual personalities.

Discussion Questions:

1. Who do you think is most qualified for the position in the Trade Winds company? Who do you think should get the job? Why do you think so?
2. Why do you think the other people are not as suitable?
3. Which qualification is the most important? Why?
4. Which qualification is the least important? Why?

5. Name some accessories for women. How many of these things do you have?
6. Name some accessories for men. How many of these things do you have?
7. Can you type? About how many WPM? Do you often type? What do you type?
8. With which countries does your country do international trade?
9. What things does your country import? Why? What things does it export? Why?
10. Which of the applicants' majors are you interested in?
11. Which other subjects are you interested in? Why?
12. Which of the subjects are you not interested in? Why?
13. Have you ever applied for a job? Which job? Did you get the job? Did you like it?

14. Which jobs are you interested in? Why?
12. Which jobs are you not interested in? Why?
13. What kind of jobs do your family members have?
14. Which of these jobs are you interested in?
15. Would you like to work for an international trade company? Why?
16. What is your ideal job? What is your ideal salary?
17. Some people get raises at work. What can you do to get a raise?
18. Some people get promotions at work. What can you do to get a promotion?
19. Some people get jobs and promotions because of family connections. This means someone in their family helps them to get a job. How do you feel about this?
20. Do you know anyone who got his or her job because of family connections? Who?

Different people have different kinds of careers. There are many different kinds of careers and jobs to choose from. People have a wide choice of occupations they can do. Different careers require different kinds of responsibilities and duties. Different careers require different kinds of skills and abilities. They have different educational requirements and qualifications. Not everyone is suitable for every kind of career.

Think about these different careers. What kinds of skills and abilities does each one require? What educational requirements do they have? What kinds of responsibilities and duties do people who do these kinds of jobs have?

- Veterinarian   - Software designer   - Police officer   - Pilot   - Author

Read about five people and their careers.

George: Hi, I'm George. I'm a veterinarian. I like to help sick animals. I need to be able to use a lot of tools and instruments in my job. Sometimes I have to do operations on animals. Other times I need to check their condition or give them an injection. After high school, I went to college for four years. My major was animal biology. After college, I went to veterinary school for four years. Now, I have my own animal clinic. I really enjoy my job. I like working with animals and enjoy talking to their owners.

Claudia: Hi, my name is Claudia. I'm a computer software designer. I design computer software. I use a computer everyday at work. I have to type a lot of information. I also need to think about how to solve a variety of complicated problems. After high school I went to college for four years. My major was computer science. After college, I found a job in a software company. I have worked there for ten years. I like my job. I like to use my imagination to design new programs and to edit old ones.

Graham: Hi, my name is Graham. I'm a police officer. My job is to help people. I drive a patrol car. Sometimes we have to arrest people who break the law and take them to the police station. After high school, I went to police college for four years. After college, I got a job in the police force in a city near where my parents live. I have been a police officer for twenty years. I really love my job. Being a police officer is very rewarding. I like to help people. I feel I am doing something worthwhile.

Bruce: Hi, my name is Bruce. I'm a pilot. My job is to fly an airplane. I usually fly international routes from the USA to Europe. After high school, I joined the Air Force. In the Air Force I learned how to fly planes. I was in the Air Force for fifteen years. After the Air Force, I got a job as a commercial pilot with a big airline. I have worked there for about nine years. I love my job. It is exciting and I enjoy traveling.

Melissa: Hi, my name is Melissa. I'm an author. I write children's books. I usually write about three or four books a year. I write stories for children in elementary school. I also do my own illustrations. After high school I went to college. My major was elementary education. After college, I went to graduate school. My major was English literature. I love writing children's stories. I like to be creative and use my imagination.

Comprehension Questions:

1. What is George's job?
2. What does he need to use?
3. What does he need to do?
4. What did he do after high school?
5. Does he like his job? Why?

6. What is Claudia's job?
7. What does she have to do at work?
8. What did she do after high school?
9. What was her major?
10. What did she do after college?
11. Does she like her job? Why?

12. What is Graham's job?
13. What does he have to do at work?
14. What did he do after high school?
15. What did he do after college?
16. How does he feel about his job?

17. What does Bruce do?
18. Where does he usually fly?
19. What did he do after high school?
20. How long has he been a pilot?
21. Does he like his job? Why?

22. What is Melissa's job?
23. What does she do?
24. What did she do after high school?
25. What were her majors?
26. Does she like her job? Why?

Discussion Questions:

1. George is a veterinarian. He loves animals. Do you love animals? Which ones?
2. Which animals do you dislike? Why do you dislike them?
3. Claudia works with computers. Do you have a computer? What do you use it for?
4. How do you feel about computers? Why are they useful?
5. Graham is a police officer. Would you like to have his job? Why?
6. What dangers might a police officer have to face in his job?
7. Bruce is a pilot. Would you like to have his job? Why?
8. Have you ever been on an airplane? Where did you go? How long was the flight?
9. Melissa is an author. Would you like to have her job? Why?
10. What kinds of books did you like to read when you were a child?

11. Which of the five careers most appeals to you? Why?
12. Which of the five careers does not appeal to you? Why?
13. If you had to choose one of the five careers, which one would you choose? Why?

Lesson 5   Matt and Lucy's Wedding

- Are you married? Did you have a big wedding?
- How much does a wedding usually cost?
- Do you think big weddings are worth the money?
- Who should pay for the wedding?
- What is a good wedding gift?
- When did you last go to a wedding?
- Where was it? Who got married?

Read about Matt and Lucy's wedding.

Lucy and Matt had a big wedding. They were married on a Saturday at Unity Church. The night before the wedding they had a rehearsal. Then, the wedding party went to a restaurant for the rehearsal dinner. Matt's parents paid for the dinner. The next day was the wedding. Matt was a little nervous. The church was filled with friends and relatives. Matt and Lucy sent out over 100 invitations. The ushers were busy seating the guests.

The organist started playing the music. The bridesmaids started walking down the aisle one by one. They wore peach dresses. The groom and the groomsmen waited by the altar. They wore black tuxedos. Then, the flower girl and ring bearer walked down the aisle. Finally, the bride Lucy walked down the aisle. She wore a white wedding dress. The minister asked them to say their vows. Then, they exchanged rings.

After the wedding, the bride and groom got into a limousine and went to the reception. The reception was at a hotel. They had a big dinner. There was a tall wedding cake and a DJ played music. Everybody danced after dinner. The bride threw the bouquet to the women. The groom threw the bride's garter to the men. Whoever catches the bouquet and garter are next to get married. The next day, Matt and Lucy opened their wedding gifts. They thanked Lucy's parents for paying for the wedding. Then, they went on their honeymoon to Jamaica.

Comprehension Questions:

1. Where did Matt and Lucy get married?
2. Who went to the rehearsal dinner?
3. Who paid for the rehearsal dinner?
4. How did Matt feel on his wedding day?
5. Who seated the guests?
6. How many invitations did Matt and Lucy send out?
7. Who walked down the aisle first?
8. Where were the groomsmen waiting?
9. Who asked Matt and Lucy to say their vows?
10. Where did everyone go after the wedding?
11. How did Matt and Lucy get to the reception?
12. What did everybody do after dinner?
13. What did the bride throw?
14. What did the groom throw?
15. Who paid for the wedding?
16. Where did Matt and Lucy go on their honeymoon?

Discussion Questions:

1. Can a wedding be too big or too expensive?
2. What is your idea for a perfect wedding?
3. Should the bride's family pay for the wedding?
4. Do you wear a wedding ring?
5. Would you like your husband or wife to wear a ring? Why?
6. Should marriage be forever?
7. Should gays and lesbians be able to get married?

8. Why do people get married?
9. What do brides and grooms wear in your country?
10. How old do you have to be to get married?
11. What age is too young to get married? Why?
12. What do you think about eloping?
13. Would you marry someone your parents didn't like?

14. Describe a traditional wedding in your country.
15. Is it okay for a couple to live together before marriage?
16. Is it okay to have a baby before you get married?
17. What do you think of arranged marriages?

18. Where are some good honeymoon destinations?
19. Where would be your ideal honeymoon destination? Why?
20. Why do people sometimes get divorced?
21. What are some alternatives to divorce? How can a couple save their marriage?

Lesson 6 **Funerals**

- Have you ever been to a funeral?
- Whose funerals have you been to? How did your feel?
- Why do people have funerals?
- Why do some people dislike going to funerals?
- Are people in your country usually buried or cremated?
- Would you prefer to be buried or cremated? Why?
- Do you like going to graveyards? Why or why not?

Read the article below about a funeral.

It was Sunday morning and Sue was eating breakfast. The phone rang. It was her mother. She told Sue her Uncle Bill had died of a heart attack. Sue felt very sad. Her mother told her that his body was taken to Simms Funeral Home on 7th Avenue. She said there would be a visitation (or wake) on Tuesday night at the funeral home. The funeral service would be at Free Church on Wednesday morning.

On Tuesday morning, Sue called the florist. She sent flowers to the funeral home and a sympathy card. She went to the market and bought a newspaper. She wanted to read the obituary. The obituary or death notice told about her uncle's life and had a picture of him. It told how many children he had and who his relatives were. It also said where the visitation and funeral were being held.

Sue put on a dark colored dress and drove to the visitation. There were many people waiting in line to see the family. They wanted to give their condolences. Uncle Bill's casket was open for a viewing. Uncle Bill did not want to be cremated, he wanted to be buried. Sue waited in line and talked to the family. She told them she was sorry for their loss. The family thanked Sue for the sympathy card and flowers.

The next day, Sue went to Free Church for the funeral service. Some of Uncle Bill's friends spoke about his life. Then, everyone drove their cars to the cemetery. They all followed the hearse.   Afterwards, there was a big lunch for all the family and friends at Bill's brother's house. They all talked about Bill and how sorry they were that he had passed away. They all had very fond memories of him. They will all miss Bill.

Comprehension Questions:

1. When did Uncle Bill die?
2. How did Uncle Bill die?
3. Who told Sue her uncle died?
4. Where was the body taken?
5. When was the visitation?
6. When was the funeral service?
7. What did Sue send on Tuesday morning?
8. Why did she buy a newspaper?
9. What did the obituary say?
10. What did Sue wear to the visitation?
11. Why were people waiting in line?
12. Was Uncle Bill cremated?
13. What did Sue tell the family?
14. Why did the family thank Sue?
15. Where was the funeral service?
16. What did everyone follow?
17. Where did everyone go after the funeral?
18. What did they do there?
19. Who will miss Bill?
20. What kinds of memories do they all have?

Discussion Questions:

1. When did you last feel sympathy for someone?
2. What do people wear to funerals in your country?
3. Are there funeral homes in your country?
4. Where do most people have funerals?

5. Is being cremated popular in your country?
6. How long do people wait before they are buried?
7. Are obituaries printed in your country's newspapers?
8. What are the funeral customs in your country?
9. How are they different from some American customs?

10. Talk about a funeral you attended.
11. Do you feel uncomfortable going to funerals?
12. Are funerals expensive in your country?
13. Who usually pays for funerals in your country?
14. Do you send flowers to the family of the person who died?
15. Do you ever send anything else? What do you send?

16. When was the last time you went to a graveyard? Why did you go there?
17. Do you feel graveyards are sentimental, moving places or scary, spooky places?
18. Would you prefer to be buried or cremated? Why?
19. If you were cremated, where would you like to put your ashes? Why?
20. Are there any other choices besides being buried or cremated?

Lesson 7 — Colors

- What is your favorite color? Why?
- What colors do you dislike? Why?
- What colors put you in a good mood?
- What colors put you in a bad mood?
- What colors do you have in your house?
- Have you ever seen a rainbow? Where?

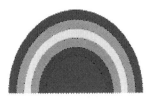

The following story is based on a Native American legend.

Once upon a time the colors of the world started to fight. They all believed that they were the best, the most important, the most useful, and the favorite. Green said, "Clearly I am the most important. I am the sign of life and of hope. I was chosen for grass, leaves, and trees. Without me, all animals would die. Look out over the countryside and you will see that I am in the majority." Blue interrupted and said, "You only think about the Earth, but consider the sky and sea. Water is the basis of life. The sky gives space, peace, and serenity. Without my peace, you would all be nothing."

Yellow laughed and said, "You are all so serious. I bring laughter and warmth to the world. The sun is yellow, the moon is yellow, and the stars are yellow. Every time you look at a sunflower, the whole world starts to smile. Without me, there would be no fun." Orange started to get angry. "I am the color of health and strength. I am important because I serve the needs of human life. I carry the most important vitamins. Think about carrots, pumpkins, oranges, and mangos. I don't hang around all the time, but when I fill the sky at sunrise or sunset, my beauty is so striking that no one gives another thought to any of you."

Finally, red shouted, "I am the ruler of all of you! I am blood! Life's blood! I am the color of danger and bravery. I am also the color of passion, love, the red rose, and the poinsettia. Without me, the earth would be as empty as the moon!" Purple spoke up and said, "I am the color of royalty and power. Kings, chiefs, and bishops have always chosen me because I am a sign of authority and wisdom. People do not question me, they listen and obey." Finally, indigo spoke, much more quietly than all the others, but with just as much determination. "Think of me. I am the color of silence. You hardly notice me, but without me you all mean nothing. I represent thought and reflection, twilight and deep water. You need me for balance and contrast, for prayer and inner peace."

The colors went on fighting until they became louder and louder. Suddenly, there was a startling flash of bright lightening. Thunder rolled and boomed. Then, rain started to pour down. The colors crouched down in fear and the rain began to speak. "You colors are all foolish. Don't you know that you were each made for a special purpose? Join hands and come with me."

The colors all joined hands and the rain stretched them across the sky. The rain continued, "From now on, when it rains, each of you will stretch across the sky in a great bow of colors as a reminder that you can all live in peace."

Comprehension Questions:

1. Why did the colors of the world start to fight?
2. What did green say?
3. Where can you see green as a majority?
4. What color are the sky and sea?
5. What does the sky do?
6. What does yellow bring to the world?
7. What color is a sunflower?
8. Why is orange important for our health?
9. What color is a pumpkin?
10. What is the color of danger and bravery?
11. What is the color of royalty?
12. What would the world be like without red?
13. What is the color for prayer and inner peace?
14. Which color spoke the quietest?
15. What happened when the colors continued fighting?
16. What did the colors do when the rain started to speak?
17. What did the rain say?
18. What did the colors do?
19. What did the colors make together?
20. What will the rainbow remind them?

Discussion Questions:

1. What is your favorite color? Why? Where can you see this color?
2. What color clothing do you usually wear? Why?
3. What color clothing are you wearing right now?
4. What color clothing do you never wear? Why?
5. What color is your bedroom? Living room?
6. What color is your hair?
7. If you could change the color of your hair, what color would you like? Why?

8. What does black usually symbolize? Why?
9. How does red make you feel? What are some things that are red?
10. What color is your car? Did you choose the color? Why did you choose this color?
11. What color is considered lucky? Why? Are any colors considered unlucky?
12. Name the colors of the rainbow.
13. What are the colors on the flag in your country? What do they symbolize?
14. What color makes you feel happy? Sad? Relaxed?
15. What do you do when you are sad? How do you make yourself feel better?

16. Name some things that are green. Where can you see them?
17. Name some things that are yellow. Where can you see them?
18. Name some things that are white. Where can you see them?
19. Which colors are romantic? Where can we see these romantic colors?
20. What were your school's colors? Did you like these colors? Why?

Color Idioms

Colors can be used to express different kinds of feelings and situations. Look at these different English idioms that use color. An idiom is a commonly used phrase. Do you know what they mean? Try to match the idiom with its meaning.

Color Idiom:	Meaning:
He was <u>tickled pink.</u>	Go out and have a good time.
I see him only <u>once in a blue moon.</u>	Fired notice.
His neighbor was <u>green with envy.</u>	Very healthy.
Their business <u>is in the red.</u>	A lie that doesn't hurt anyone.
They hope it will be <u>in the</u> black next year.	Power failure.
I <u>see red</u> when people litter.	Very afraid.
Mondays always make me <u>feel blue.</u>	Very happy.
The doctor told me <u>I was in the pink.</u>	With great success.
Last night we had <u>a black out.</u>	Become angry.
She passed her exams <u>with flying colors.</u>	Very jealous of someone.
The boy told the teacher <u>a white lie.</u>	Feel depressed.
John got <u>a pink slip</u> from work last week.	Making a profit.
Let's <u>paint the town red</u> this weekend.	Losing money.
He was <u>as white as a ghost.</u>	Very seldom, almost never.

Fill in the blanks with the correct color idiom.

1. My sister became _____ when she saw the man at the window.

2. When my cousin came to visit us, we decided to go out and _____.

3. I received my _____ last week and I am now looking for a new job.

4. I told my boss a _____. I said I was sick yesterday but actually I wasn't.

5. She passed her course _____ and wants to go out and celebrate.

6. He really _____ last night when I told him I wouldn't come to work today.

7. The company has been _____ since they began to cut costs.

8. The company has been _____ since their exports decreased by 35 per cent.

9. I was _____ when I heard that she would be going to London for a week.

10. We go out for Italian food _____ although we enjoy it.

11. She was_____ when you visited her.

12. There was a _____ in our house last night. We had to use candles.

13. I need to have a physical exam next week. I hope I am _____.

14. My classmate is _____. I hope I can cheer her up.

Discussion Questions:

1. When was the last time you were tickled pink? What happened?
2. What things make you happy? What things make you unhappy?
3. What things do you do only once in a blue moon? Why do you do them so seldom?
4. Have you ever been green with envy? Who were you envious of?
5. Has anybody ever been envious of you? Why?
6. Which local businesses are in the red? Why is their business successful?
7. Which local businesses are in the black? Why is their business unsuccessful?
8. What things make you see red?
9. When was the last time you were really angry? What happened?
10. What things make you feel blue?

11. When was the last time you were really sad? What happened?
12. Do you think you are in the pink? How is your health?
13. When was the last time you were sick? What did you do?
14. Have you ever been in a black out? What happened?
15. How can you prepare for a blackout?
16. Have you ever passed an exam with flying colors?
17. Do you like to take exams? Why?

18. Have you ever told anyone a white lie? Why?
19. Why do people tell white lies?
20. Do you know anyone who has received a pink slip?
21. How would you like to paint the town red?
22. Do you like to drink alcohol? Why?
23. Have you ever been as white as a ghost?
24. What things are you afraid of? Why are you afraid of them?
25. When was the last time you were really scared? What happened?

Lesson 9   Etiquette and Good Manners

- Do you have good manners? Are you a polite person?
- Is it proper etiquette to arrive late to work or school?
- Do you think of others before you think of yourself?
- How do people learn good manners?
- What do you do when someone is rude?

Read about some American manners and etiquette.

Etiquette and manners are basic rules to follow in everyday social situations. Etiquette rules show you polite and appropriate behavior. Manners teach you to consider others before you think of yourself and to be polite to others. Etiquette and good manners change from country to country. You may find that etiquette in your country is more conservative than the etiquette of other countries. You may also find that sometimes your country's etiquette and manners are more liberal than those of other countries.

There was once an English queen who welcomed a sea captain to her dinner table. Instead of picking up his soupspoon and scooping from the back of the bowl to the front, he picked up the entire bowl and began drinking from it. To make him feel comfortable, the queen picked up her bowl and began drinking in the same way. This is an example of bad etiquette and good manners. The sea captain showed poor etiquette because of his soup-eating style. The queen showed good manners by not making the captain feel uncomfortable.

In America there are many rules and guidelines for living everyday life. Here are a few of those guidelines for behaving politely in American society.

Polite Etiquette: You should...	Impolite Etiquette: You shouldn't...
RSVP for parties	Arrive late.
Cover your mouth when you sneeze or cough.	Burp loudly in a public place. If you have to, cover your mouth.
Tell someone quietly that they have something in their teeth.	Pick your nose in a public place.
Tip at bars and restaurants.	Put your elbows on the dinner table.
Send thank-you notes when you receive a gift.	Talk with your mouth full of food.
Wait your turn in line.	Never talk out of turn. Wait for your chance to speak.
Say please and thank-you.	Stop by someone's house without calling.

Comprehension Questions:

1. What are etiquette and manners?
2. What do these rules show you?
3. Did the sea captain display poor manners or poor etiquette?
4. Why did the English queen drink from her bowl instead of using her spoon?
5. What should you do if you are invited to a party?
6. What shouldn't you do at a party?
7. What should you do if you cough?
8. What shouldn't you do in a public place?
9. What should you do if someone has something in his or her teeth?
10. Where should you leave a tip?
11. What shouldn't you do at the dinner table?
12. What should you do when you receive a gift?
13. What shouldn't you do when you are eating?
14. What should you do when you are in a line?
15. What should you do when someone is speaking?
16. What should you remember to say?
17. What should you do if you want to visit someone?

Discussion Questions:

1. Is etiquette in your country similar to or different from American etiquette?
2. Are you a polite person? Give an example.
3. Have you ever met someone who was rude? Who? Where?
4. Have you ever noticed that you were being rude to someone? What did you do?
5. Do people like to wait in line in your country?
6. If someone cuts in front of you in a line, what would you do?
7. Do you think people should have better driving etiquette?
8. How should you treat your mother and father? Grandmother and grandfather?
9. How should you treat your teacher? How should you treat your boss?
10. How do you feel about cell phone etiquette? Why should you turn your phone off before a movie or while you are in class?
11. If you were at a movie people were talking loudly, what would you do?
12. How often do you hold the door open for the person behind you?
13. How do we learn good etiquette and polite manners?
14. Think about etiquette in your country. Make a list of polite and impolite behavior.

Polite: You should...	Impolite: You shouldn't...

Lesson 10 — Dining Etiquette

- Do you prefer to eat out or eat at home? Why?
- Is eating out expensive in your country?
- Do you prefer formal or casual dinners? Why?
- What is dining etiquette? Are you a polite eater?
- When was the last time you went out to eat?
- Where did you go? What kind of food did you eat?

Read about dining etiquette.

Did you know that the point of etiquette rules is to make you feel comfortable, not uncomfortable? If there are rules that people follow, it takes the guesswork out of public behavior. When dining at a formal restaurant, deciding which drinking glass is yours can be confusing. This is one of the first decisions to make at the dinner table. Here is an easy tip to help you remember. Hold both hands in front of you, palms facing each other. Using the tips of your thumb and forefinger, make circles on each hand. The remaining three fingers in each hand point upwards. Your left hand will form a "b" and your right hand will form a "d". Bread (b) is on the left, and drink (d) is on the right. If your neighbor has taken your bread plate or glass, quietly ask the waiter for another.

Napkins belong in your lap. Large napkins can be folded in half. They should never be tucked into your shirt like a bib. Wait for the host to unfold his napkin before unfolding yours. In a banquet setting or at a restaurant, simply place your napkin on your lap as soon as you are seated. If you excuse yourself from the table, loosely fold the napkin and place it to the left or right of your plate. Do not hang it over the back of your chair. Do not refold your napkin or wad it up on the table either.

General Dining Etiquette Tips:

- Start eating hot food when it is served, do not wait for everyone else to begin.
- For soup, dip the spoon into the soup, from the edge of the bowl to the center, moving away from you. Sip, not slurp, from the edge of the spoon.
- It is proper to tip a soup bowl slightly to get all of the soup.
- Never turn the glass upside down to decline wine. It is more polite to let the wine be poured and not draw attention to yourself. If you are asked about wine and will not be drinking, quietly decline.
- Do not ask for a doggy bag unless it is an informal dining situation.
- Do not smoke at the table.
- Do not ask to taste someone else's food.
- Do not talk with your mouth full.
- Chew with your mouth closed.
- If soup is too hot to eat, let it cool in the bowl. Do not blow on it.
- Practice good posture. If not eating, place your hand in your lap or rest your wrists on the edge of the table. Do not put your elbows on the table.

Comprehension Questions:

1. What is the point of dining etiquette rules?
2. What is the first decision you make at the dinner table?
3. Which side is your drinking glass on, the left or the right?
4. Where does your napkin belong?
5. If you leave the table, where should you put your napkin?
6. When do you start eating hot food?
7. Is it okay to slurp your soup?
8. If you do not want to drink wine, what should you do?
9. If your soup is too hot, what should you do?
10. Should you talk with your mouth full of food?
11. How should you chew your food?
12. Is it proper to taste someone else's food?
13. Is it okay to smoke at the dinner table?
14. When is it okay to ask for a doggy bag?
15. Is it proper to put your elbows on the table?

Discussion Questions:

1. What is the difference between formal and casual dining?
2. Have you ever been to a formal dinner party? Where was it? What did you have?
3. Would you rather go out for a formal dinner or a casual dinner? Why?
4. What would you wear to a formal dinner party?
5. What would you wear to a casual dinner party?
6. Who usually sits at the head of the table?
7. Have you ever been the host or hostess of a party? If so, was it formal or casual?
8. What are the duties of a host?

9. What kinds of food would you put salt and pepper on?
10. What is the difference between lunch and supper?
11. How does one propose a toast?
12. What are the duties of a waiter or waitress?
13. What would you say to a guest who told you he did not like the meal you cooked?

14. If you were invited to a dinner party and you didn't like the food what would you do if the host or hostess asked you: *"How is the food?"*

15. Name some casual restaurants that you know. Name some formal restaurants.

Casual restaurants	Formal restaurants

Lesson 11   Eating Out: Fast Food

- Do you like American style fast food? Why or Why not?
- How often to you go to McDonald's? KFC? Subway?
- Do you ever order pizza? From where?
- McDonald's, KFC, and Domino's are franchise restaurants. Would you like to own one? Why or why not?
- Do you think eating fast food is healthy? Why or why not?
- What is your favorite restaurant?

Read about American fast food.

Americans eat a lot of fast food. There are fast food restaurants in every city throughout the United States. Americans like fast food for a variety of reasons. Convenience is the main reason why people eat fast food. Everyone has a busy schedule and most people don't have time to cook. Fast food restaurants provide quick service at low prices. Dinner can be eaten in the car as you drive from work to English class.

Fast food also comes in a variety of choices. Taco Bell serves Mexican fast food. Happy Wok serves Chinese fast food and at Little Italy, you can buy Italian fast food. When you need to eat in a hurry, there are many different kinds of fast food to choose from. Shopping malls are usually the best place to see an example of this variety. Large shopping malls have a food court. This is an area inside the mall where you can pick any kind of food that you want. You can eat hamburgers, hotdogs, pizza, fried rice or ice cream. The choices are endless.

The most familiar name in fast food is McDonald's. You can travel most anywhere in the world and there are two names that everyone knows. One is Michael Jordan and the other is McDonald's. McDonald's began as a 'burger joint'. They only sold hamburgers and French fries. The first restaurant opened in 1948. By 1982, the McDonald's Corporation earned about $7 billion. Why was it so successful?

People like McDonald's food. The French fries are tasty and they are even better when you dip them in ketchup. The burgers are thin and easy to gobble down. On a hot day, you can sip on a milk shake or have a hot fudge sundae. McDonald's also adjusts their menu from country to country. In Taiwan they serve corn soup and in Italy you can buy a slice of pizza.

Overall, fast food is becoming more and more popular. People are busy and they need to eat. Fast food restaurants cater to this need. It makes lives easier by cooking your breakfast, lunch or dinner for you. People like fast food but is it really good for us?

Comprehension Questions:

1. What is the main reason why people like fast food?
2. What do fast food restaurants provide?
3. What kinds of fast food can you buy?
4. What kind of food does Taco Bell serve?
5. What is a food court?
6. What kind of food can you eat at a food court?
7. What is the most familiar name in fast food?
8. When did the first McDonald's restaurant open?
9. Was the first McDonald's a 'burger joint'?
10. What did they serve?
11. How much money did the McDonald's Corporation earn in 1982?
12. Why do people like McDonald's food?
13. How does McDonald's try to please everyone around the world?
14. How does fast food make lives easier?
15. Is fast food really good for us?

Discussion Questions:

1. Have you ever been to McDonald's? If so, what did you order? Did you like it?
2. Do you think working at a fast food restaurant is a good job? Why?
3. Do you know anyone who works at McDonald's? Do they like their job?
4. Why do people go to fast food restaurants?
5. What are some advantages of fast food restaurants? Disadvantages?

6. Do you think people are getting fatter by eating too much fast food?
7. Are you a busy person? If so, how can fast food make your life easier?
8. Is it a good idea for parents to feed their children American style fast food? Why?
9. What kind of food should parents give their children to eat? Why?
10. How often do you eat food from street vendors? What do you eat?
11. Is food from street vendors usually healthy or unhealthy?   Why do people eat it?
12. What other kinds of fast food is popular in your country?

| Cheeseburger | French Fries | Pizza |

Would you like to eat these? Why or why not?

Eating Out: Restaurants

- What kind of restaurants do you like to go to?
- How often do you go out to eat?
- What is your favorite restaurant?
- Why do you like this one so much?
- Do you like trying new foods? Why?
- Do you like Western food? What kind?
- Do you like any other international food? What?
- What kind of food do you dislike the most? Why?

Read some different restaurant advertisements.

Chen's Chow Mein	Lino's Pizzeria	Alvarez Mexican	The Irish Rose
We serve lunch and dinner. Enjoy traditional Cantonese style food. Dim sum, chow mein and seafood specials. Children under 12 pay what they weigh.	We boast the best pizza in town. If you don't like pizza, try our spaghetti with mama's special sauce. Live bands on Saturday nights.	Tacos, burritos, and nachos. Dine in or take out. Try a margarita on the patio while you wait. Sunday Special: All you can eat Mexican buffet for $5.00.	Fine dining at its best. Steaks and seafood. Let us prepare your perfect dining experience as you sip the finest wines in town. Irish beer on draft and Irish whiskey on the shelf.
Open daily from 11:30 AM until 11:00 PM Closed on Mondays	Open 7 days a week from 2 PM until 2 AM	Open daily from 11:30 AM until 1:30 AM	Open Tuesday-Saturday. 5 PM until 2 AM Reservations only
123 Second Street 655-1212	65 State Street 877-5432	878 London Ave. 654-5412	962 Market Street 987-1789

Comprehension Questions:

1. What's the name of the Italian restaurant?
2. What kind of food does Alvarez serve?
3. At which restaurant can you sit outside?
4. Are any of these places open 24 hours?
5. Which restaurant requires a reservation?
6. Which restaurant serves pasta?
7. Can you get chow mein at Alvarez?
8. What does Lino's boast?
9. What day is Chen's closed?
10. Where is the Irish Rose?
11. What is Chen's phone number?
12. What kind of alcoholic beverages does the Irish Rose have?
13. What time does Chen's open? Close?
14. What is the Sunday special at Alvarez?
15. What day is the Irish Rose closed?
16. Which restaurant has a special for children? What is it?

Discussion Questions:

1. Which of the four restaurants would you prefer to try? Why?
2. Which one would you least like to try? Why?
3. If you traveled to America, what kind of food would you like to try?
4. If you traveled to Europe what kind of food would you like to try?
5. If you traveled to China what kind of food would you like to try?
6. If you traveled to India what kind of food would you like to try?

7. If you moved overseas, would you cook at home or eat out?
8. Which are easier to use: a knife and fork or chopsticks?
9. What things are on the table in a restaurant?

10. How do you usually dress when you go out to eat? Casual or formal?
11. Is western food more or less healthy than the food in your country? How?
12. Which restaurants in your city are considered to be fine dining?
13. What is the most expensive restaurant in your city? Is it worth the price?
14. What is a good time to go out for dinner? Early or late?
15. Do restaurants in your country offer an 'early bird' special?

16. Have you ever worked in a restaurant? If so, describe your experience?
17. Do people usually tip in your country? How do you feel about tipping?
18. What kinds of people work in a restaurant?
19. Have you ever found a fly in your soup? If so, what would you do?
20. What would you do if the chef burned your food?

21. If your teacher cooked you dinner, what do you think he/she would cook?
22. If you cooked dinner for your teacher, what would you cook? Why?

Lesson 13   Earthquakes

- Which areas of the world often have earthquakes?
- Where have serious earthquakes happened recently?
- Have you ever felt a strong earthquake?
- What happens during an earthquake?
- What kind of damage can earthquakes cause?
- What should you do if you are in an earthquake?
- What should you not do if you are in an earthquake?

Read about earthquakes.

Earthquakes occur when shifting pieces of the Earth's surface cause the ground to shudder. Sometimes there are disastrous results. Earthquakes have killed countless numbers of people and tossed their buildings around like toys. About 35 earthquakes are observed around the globe every day, and about 18 major ones happen every year.

Earthquakes can happen anywhere. A series of quakes near the town of New Madrid, Missouri, during the winter of 1811-1812 was felt as far north as Canada, as far south as the Gulf of Mexico, and rattled chinaware in Washington, D.C. Because the American Midwest was so sparsely populated, the death toll was light. Today, New Madrid lies within 150 miles (240 kilometers) of two major cities: St. Louis, Missouri, and Memphis, Tennessee. When a Midwestern earthquake happens again, as experts say it surely will, the toll in human life and property destruction is expected to be high.

Earthquakes happen very suddenly. Subterranean forces cause gigantic plates of rock to shudder as they slip past each other. The major cause of earthquakes is shifting tectonic plates. Tectonic plates are the fragments of crust that float on the Earth's thick mantle. Most earthquakes occur at the boundaries of these plates. The Ring of Fire in the Pacific Ocean is an example of a boundary earthquake. Mid-plate earthquakes, like the one at New Madrid, are usually large and destructive.

Damage from earthquakes is not limited to buildings, bridges, and dams. They can trigger fires and landslides. When loose soil, such as landfill, loses its ability to bear loads, the ground behaves like quicksand. Buildings can sink and even disappear.

When they happen at sea, earthquakes can generate seismic waves called tsunamis. Tsunamis travel great distances at speeds equaling those of commercial jetliners. They are barely noticeable and often appear as ripples on the surface of the water. When they approach shores, they become monsters.

Since earthquakes will happen whether they are predicted or not, communities in many earthquake-prone areas such as southern California have upgraded building codes to make their structures less susceptible to damage. Japan has invested heavily in earthquake-proofing buildings in such areas as downtown Tokyo. They hope to save lives and property before the next earthquake happens.

Comprehension Questions:

1. Why do earthquakes occur?
2. How many earthquakes are observed every day?
3. How many major earthquakes occur every year?
4. Where can earthquakes happen?
5. What happened in New Madrid during the winter of 1811-1812?
6. Where does New Madrid lie today?
7. What do experts fear if another earthquake should occur?
8. What causes plates of rock to shudder?
9. What is the major cause of earthquakes?
10. Where do most earthquakes occur?
11. Where is the Ring of Fire?
12. What is the difference between a mid-plate and boundary earthquake?
13. What can happen to the ground during an earthquake?
14. What can happen when earthquakes occur at sea?
15. What happens when tsunamis reach the shore?
16. What have communities in many earthquake-prone areas done?
17. What has Japan done?
18. What does Japan hope to do?

Discussion Questions:

1. Do earthquakes often occur in your country? Where do they usually occur?
2. Have you ever felt a strong earthquake? What did it feel like? How did you feel?
3. Do you think earthquakes are exciting or scary? Why?
4. Where have some major earthquakes occurred? What happened to these places?
5. Which is more valuable: human life or property? Why?
6. How can you make your home more earthquake-safe?
7. If an earthquake occurs what should you do? What should you not do?
8. Disaster victims often need a lot of help. They rely on people to donate things that they need. What would you be willing to donate to victims of an earthquake?

Money?   Blood?   Clothes?   Food?   Blankets?   Toiletries?   Time?

9. Imagine that your home was damaged in an earthquake. You have to evacuate your city and move to a safe place in the countryside for a while. What will you take with you? Look at this list. Which things are important? Which things are not important?

Tools	Food	Clothing	Equipment	Others
Flashlight	Canned meat	Jacket	Matches	Books
Batteries	Canned fruit	Sweater	First-aid kit	Magazines
Swiss army knife	Vegetables	Shorts and T-shirts	Mirror	Bicycle
Shovel	Salt and sugar	Boots	Cell phone	Walkman
Compass	Instant noodles	Sandals	Camera	Diary
Magnifying glass	Coffee	Raincoat	Alarm clock	Umbrella

10. Are there any other things that you would want to take? What are they?

Lesson 14 — Emergency: Fires

- How can you make a fire?
- How do household fires begin?
- How can you prevent household fires?
- How can you put out a small household fire?
- What should you do if there is a big fire?
- What shouldn't you do if there is a fire?

Read about fires.

Household fires can begin for many reasons. They can start when someone forgets to put out a cigarette. Fires can also start because of a gas leak. Sometimes gas tanks are faulty. Fires can start in the kitchen. Sometimes people use oil when they cook and this can catch fire if you are not careful. Fires can start due to faulty electrical wires or a broken appliance. Sometimes fires start due to people being careless with matches or a lighter. It is important that people remember to be very careful when handling fire or anything that could cause a fire. Most household fires start because people are careless and irresponsible. We need to remember to be extra careful during winter. In the winter the air is usually very dry and this makes it more likely that fires will start. This also means that if fires start they can get out of control more easily and become serious emergencies.

In case of a household fire it is important to be prepared. Every home should have a fire extinguisher and a smoke detector. Both of these are quite cheap and easy to find. You can buy them at a hardware store. A smoke detector will make a noise when it senses smoke. They are easy to install. Just screw them to the ceiling and make sure the batteries are fresh. You can easily put out small household fires with a fire extinguisher. Make sure that everyone in the family knows how to use it. Read the instructions and test it to make sure that it works.

In case of big fires, you should call the fire department. Everyone in the family should know the fire department's telephone number. The fire department will send a fire truck and firefighters to come and put out the fire. It is important to get everyone out of the house as quickly as possible. The most important thing to remember is to stay calm and don't panic. People who panic in a fire can get hurt easily.

Sometimes fires are caused by arson. Arson is the deliberate burning of property, and it is a very serious crime. Arson causes 1 billion dollars damage to buildings every year in America. Arson fires also cause many serious injuries and even death. There are different reasons that people commit arson. Sometimes people commit arson for profit. This happens when people burn a building to collect the insurance money. Most buildings have fire insurance. This means that if the building burns down, the owner can collect money for the damage. People also commit arson for revenge. They do this to get even with someone they feel did something wrong to them. Children or teenagers start some fires. Sometimes they play with fire and it gets out of control. Other times they are curious about fire and they like to watch it. They like the excitement of the fire trucks, the firefighters, and the big crowds of people who usually gather to watch.

Comprehension Questions:

1. How do household fires start?
2. What should every home have in case of fire?
3. Are these things expensive?
4. Where can you buy a smoke detector?
5. What will a smoke detector do?
6. What can we use a fire extinguisher for?
7. What should you do in case of a big fire?
8. What will the fire department do?
9. What is arson?
10. Why do people commit arson?
11. Why do some children and teenagers sometimes start fires?

Discussion Questions:

1. How many doors does your house have?
2. How many balconies does your house have?
3. How many different ways can you get out of your house?
4. Do you have any fire extinguishers in your house?
5. Do you have any smoke detectors in your home?
6. Do you think it is important to have fire extinguishers?
7. Have you ever seen a fire? Where was it? What happened? Was anyone injured?
8. Do you think being a firefighter is a dangerous or an exciting job?
9. Would you like to be a firefighter? Why?
10. Do you think being a police officer is a dangerous or an exciting job?
11. Would you like to be a police officer? Why?
12. Arson is a very serious crime. What is a suitable punishment for an arsonist?
13. How do you feel when you see a fire? Do you think it is dangerous or exciting?

Imagine: You wake up in the middle of the night and smell smoke. You go downstairs and the living room is on fire! The fire is quite big and you don't have any fire extinguishers in the house. What are you going to do? Number the following things in the order that you would do them. Add one of your own ideas to the list.

1. Call the fire department
2. Wake your family members
3. Get dressed
4. Go outside
5. Grab your personal belongings
6. Look for the dog
7. Put on your shoes
8. Try to put out the fire

9. _____.

Gambling

- What is gambling? What is the point of gambling?
- What are the negative sides to gambling?
- What different kinds of gambling are there?
- Which kinds of gambling are legal?
- Which kinds of gambling are illegal?
- Which places have legalized all kinds of gambling?
- What is a casino? What kinds of gambling do casinos offer their customers?

Read about four different gamblers.

Martin, Kevin, Eileen, and Jean are all at the High Rollers Casino in Las Vegas. They are all gambling on different kinds of games. Some have won and some have lost.

Name: Martin
Age: 39
Occupation: Advertising designer
Game: Cards (Blackjack)
Record: Won $500 playing poker
Comment: "I enjoy gambling. I'll come back next month. I don't think it really harms anyone, if you're careful."

Name: Kevin
Age: 48
Occupation: Construction worker
Game: Dice
Record: Broke even
Comment: "I think gambling is okay. I rarely gamble, maybe only once or twice a year."

Name: Eileen
Age: 38
Occupation: Homemaker
Game: Slot Machine
Record: Lost $50
Comment: "I don't really like gambling at all. I just come here to accompany my husband."

Name: Jean
Age: 27
Occupation: Dental clinic assistant
Game: Roulette
Record: Lost $300
Comment: "I love gambling. I think it's a lot of fun. I enjoy coming to casinos. I think they're exciting."

Comprehension Questions:

1. Where are the four gamblers?
2. How many people won?
3. How many people lost?
4. What did Martin play?
5. Did he win or lose? How much?
6. What did Kevin play?
7. Did he win or lose? How much?
8. What did Eileen play?
9. Did she win or lose? How much?
10. What did Jean play?
11. Did she win or lose? How much?
12. Did the casino profit or lose money from these four gamblers tonight?
13. How much was the casino's total loss or profit from these four gamblers?
14. Will Martin come back? Why?
15. How often does Kevin gamble?
16. What does Eileen think about gambling?
17. Why does Jean gamble?

Discussion Questions:

1. Have you ever gambled? What have you gambled on?
2. What do you think about gambling?
3. Which kinds of gambling do you think should be legal?
4. Which kinds of gambling do you think should be illegal?
5. What kinds of gambling are popular in your country?
6. What kinds of gambling are not popular in your country?
7. Does anyone in your family gamble?
8. Do any of your friends gamble?

9. Are you usually a lucky or unlucky person?
10. What lucky things have happened to you recently?
11. What unlucky things have happened to you recently?
12. Have you ever played the lottery?

13. Imagine that you won the grand prize of the lottery: Ten million US dollars. How much will you spend? How much will you save? What will you buy? What other things will you do with the money? Fill in the chart below:

Spend / Buy	Save	Other

- What do you usually do on Friday nights?
- What do you usually do on Saturday nights?
- How often do you go out with friends?
- Where do you and friends like to go?
- Do you like going to pubs? Why?
- Do you like to go dancing? Why?
- What do your family members usually like to do on weekends? Where do they like to go?

Read about going out.

Many people like to go out on Friday and Saturday nights. Some people go out to a restaurant for dinner and then to see a movie. Other people prefer to go to a dance club or a bar. Going out with friends at night is a way for people to relax. Most people work hard all week and they like to relax on weekend nights. In America most people don't work on the weekends so they can stay out late and sleep in late the next day. The most popular day of the week is Friday and on that day you may hear many people saying, 'TGIF'. TGIF means 'Thank God it's Friday.

Pubs or bars are a good place eat, drink, dance, and meet new people. There are many different kinds of bars where people can go. If you like sports, you can go to a sports bar. If you like to listen to music you can go to a blues bar, jazz club, or piano bar. People who want to dance usually go to a dance club and if you want to drink wine you can go to a wine bar. There are also bars where you go to sit at the bar and drink while you talk with friends. The choice is up to you.

Pub Crawls are also a popular thing to do. They are organized by a group of bars and people crawl or walk from bar to bar in one evening. Sometimes there are door prizes and contests at the bars too. It is a good way to meet new people and visit the different bars in a city. Look at the following advertisement for a pub crawl.

Pub Crawl
Saturday August 19th
6pm – 2am

Crawl around to the River District hot spots!
For information call 964-6221
Pub Crawl Locations:

Irish Rose, 519 E. State St. * **Blues Tap**, 515 E. State St. * **The Office**, 513 E. State St. * **Club 505**, 505 E. State St. * **Tom's Tap**, 315 Main St. * **Auto Inn**, 310 Main St. * **Franks Sports Page**, 305 Main St. * **Big Cities Lounge**, 255 Main St. * **Shooters**, 250 Main St. * **Rocky's** 225 Main St.

Comprehension Questions:

1. When do many people like to go out?
2. What do some people like to do?
3. What do other people like to do?
4. What do many people like to do on weekend nights?
5. Why can people sleep late on weekends?
6. What is the most popular day of the week?
7. What does TGIF mean?
8. Where can you go if you like sports?
9. Where can you go if you like music?
10. Where can you go if you like dancing?
11. What is a pub crawl?
12. Who organizes pub crawls?
13. What special things do bars do during a pub crawl?
14. When is the advertised pub crawl?
15. Where is the Blues Tap Pub?
16. Where is Frank's Sports Page?
17. Where is Club 505?
18. Which two streets does this pub crawl take place on?
19. What number should you call for more information?

Discussion Questions:

1. Do you like to go to pubs? Why or why not?
2. Do you ever drink alcohol? What kind do you drink? How much can you drink?
3. Would you prefer wine, beer or whiskey?
4. What is the best way to get rid of a hangover?
5. Besides going to bars, what are other things to do on a Friday or Saturday night?
6. Pretend that you are driving around on a Friday night and you don't want to go home. Where would you go? What would you do?

7. Have you ever been to a wild party?
8. Why do police officers sometimes raid a party or a club?
9. What do you think about the nightlife in your city?
10. Is it safe to go out at night? Why or why not?
11. What kinds of people usually go to pubs?
12. Do you like to dance? Where can you go dancing?
13. What are some popular nightlife spots in your city? Do you ever go there?

14. Some parents worry about their children if they are out at night. What kinds of things do parents usually worry about?
15. Did your parents worry about you when you were younger?
16. If you have children will you worry about them? What will you worry about?
17. What time should teenagers go home on Friday and Saturday nights? Why?

Health and Fitness

- What kinds of physical activities do you do?
- Do you exercise on a regular basis? How often?
- Do you like to exercise? Why or why not?
- What are the benefits of exercise?
- Would you rather exercise at home or at a health club? Why?
- Are you overweight, underweight, or just right?

Read about staying fit.

One important part of good health is daily physical activity. There are many benefits of exercising daily. It helps keep your weight under control. It increases your ability to fall asleep quickly and sleep well. It helps strengthen your muscles, bones and lungs. It is good for your heart and gives you better circulation. It makes you feel better about yourself and helps reduce stress. Daily physical activity also reduces your risk of a heart attack and high blood pressure. These are just some of the benefits of daily exercise.

There are many activities you can do to stay fit. Jogging and swimming are popular ways of exercising. You can join a health club and do aerobics or walk on a treadmill. You can work in the garden or take a walk around your neighborhood.   Many people complain they do not have time to exercise every day.   There are some everyday activities you can do to get more exercise. You can take the stairs instead of waiting for the elevator. You can ride a bicycle instead of taking your car or scooter. You can park your car farther away from the store for a longer walk.   You can do house work instead of hiring someone to do it. These are all good ways of getting more exercise.

How often should you exercise? You should try to exercise 3 or 4 times a week. How long should you exercise? You should exercise for at least 30 minutes each time. Make exercise part of your daily routine. You should always wear comfortable clothes and shoes when exercising. You should stretch before and after exercising. You should always drink water before, during, and after you exercise. You should talk to a doctor if you are not sure what kinds of exercises are right for you.

Comprehension Questions:

1. What is an important part of good health?
2. Does exercising help you sleep better?
3. Does exercising help your hair grow?
4. Does exercising help reduce the risk of a heart attack?
5. What does exercising do for your lungs and muscles?
6. What kinds of activities can you do to stay fit?
7. What can you do at a health club?
8. What can you do instead of driving your car or scooter?
9. What can you do instead of taking the elevator?
10. What can you do instead of hiring someone to clean your house?
11. How often should you exercise?
12. What should you wear when you exercise?
13. When should you stretch?
14. What should you do before, during, and after you exercise?
15. Who should you see if you are not sure what kinds of exercises to do?

Discussion Questions:

1. Do you think you are in good shape?
2. Do you like to exercise? Why?
3. How often do you exercise? Where do you exercise?
4. What kinds of exercise do you do? Why do you do this kind?
5. When do you usually exercise? Morning, afternoon or evening?
6. Do you prefer to exercise with a friend or by yourself?
7. Do you belong to a health club? What do you do there?
8. Do you usually take the elevator or the stairs? If you wanted to go down two floors would you walk or take the elevator? Why?
9. Do you have a bicycle? How often do you ride it? Where do you go?
10. Do you like going for walks? Where are some good places to take a walk?
11. Do you think you are too busy to exercise? What are you busy doing?

- Complete this sentence: *I am usually busy* _____ *ing.*

12. Do you have any health problems? Do you often get sick?
13. Do you know anyone who has had a heart attack?
14. Does your doctor say you should get more exercise?
15. Do you ever stretch? How often do you stretch?
16. What are some ways you could get more exercise?
17. Would you rather go swimming or go jogging? Why?
18. Would you rather do aerobics or play basketball? Why?
19. Would you rather play tennis or badminton? Why?
20. Would you rather go hiking or skating? Why?

Lesson 18 DIY Immunology and Home Remedies

- What healthy things do you eat or drink?
- What unhealthy things do you eat or drink?
- What do you usually do if you feel sick?
- How is a clinic different from a hospital?
- If you need to see a doctor do you usually go to a hospital or to a clinic? Which one? Why do you go there?
- Do you often take medicine? What kind?
- Do you like the taste of vinegar? How about garlic? How about ginger?

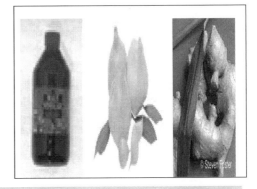

Read about how you can help your immune system to stay healthy.

Our immune system helps our body to fight diseases and helps to keep us healthy. There are many things we can do to strengthen our immune system and prevent illness. This is particularly true during the wintertime, when many people get sick from the flu, and also during outbreaks of illnesses such as the recent SARS virus. Vinegar, garlic, and ginger can help strengthen our immune system and keep us healthy. If we eat a little more vinegar, garlic and ginger, we can make our immune systems stronger. This way we can become healthier, and get sick a lot less often.

There are many different kinds of vinegars, such as fruit vinegar, lemon vinegar, plum vinegar, and rice vinegar. One good way to get enough vinegar is to mix a little with some drinking water. Keep the bottle with you and drink from it during the day. Some kinds of vinegar have a sweet taste and are nice to drink when diluted with water.

We can buy fresh garlic from a market. Just peel off the skin and slice the garlic into thin pieces. This makes an ideal spice for cooking. Garlic is both tasty and healthy. Of course, some people don't like the taste of garlic, so this method is not always suitable for everybody. It depends on whether or not you like the smell of garlic. If you don't like the smell or the taste of garlic, you can buy garlic powder in capsules at a health food store or at a pharmacy. Garlic capsules are a convenient way to get the benefits of garlic, although they can be a little expensive.

Ginger is another spice that can help to strengthen the immune system. Ginger has a sweet flavor and many people like the way it tastes. Drinking ginger tea is an excellent way to prevent getting the flu or catching a cold. If you start to feel sick, make a pot of ginger tea. Wash the ginger and slice it. Then, put some into a pan with some water. Bring this mixture to a boil, and then let it simmer. The longer you let it simmer, the stronger the tea will taste. Ginger tea can be quite strong. If the taste is too strong for you, add a little sugar to make it sweeter.

When people are sick or don't feel well they often go to see a doctor for help or they get some medicine from the drugstore. Many people also use home remedies for common illnesses. Home remedies are things we can do at home to cure an illness or minor medical problem. For example, lots of people drink hot chicken soup when they have a cold. They find that drinking chicken soup makes them feel more comfortable.

When you burn yourself you should put the burn under cold water. You can also put a cold cloth or handkerchief on it. Do not put ice on the burn. This will damage the skin even more. For a cough you can drink tea with lemon and honey. This is also good for a sore throat. For insomnia people say you should drink a glass of warm milk. This should make you feel more comfortable and help you to get to sleep.

Comprehension Questions:

1. What does our immune system do?
2. What happens when our immune system is stronger?
3. What are some different kinds of vinegar?
4. How can we make sure we get enough vinegar everyday?
5. Where can we buy fresh garlic?
6. How can we use garlic?
7. If you don't like the smell of garlic, what can you do?
8. How does ginger taste?
9. What can we do with ginger?
10. How do you make ginger tea?
11. What are home remedies?
12. What is a good home remedy for a cold?
13. What is a good home remedy for a burn?
14. What is a good home remedy for a cough?
15. What is a good home remedy for a sore throat?

Discussion Questions:

The main idea of a paragraph is what the paragraph is basically trying to tell you. In an article, each paragraph usually has one clear main idea. What is the main idea of each of the six paragraphs in the article? Write the main ideas here:

Paragraph 1: _____

Paragraph 2: _____

Paragraph 3: _____

Paragraph 4: _____

Paragraph 5: _____

Paragraph 6: _____

1. Which of the home remedies do you think is most useful? Why?
2. Which remedies would you not like to try? Why?
3. Do you know any other home remedies? What are they?
4. Do you often get sick? What kind of medical problems do you have?
5. Do you always go to see a doctor when you are sick?
6. Do you prefer the taste of garlic, ginger, or vinegar?
7. Do you ever drink ginger tea? What other kinds of tea do you like to drink?

Remodeling a Home

- What is D.I.Y.? Have you ever done any D.I.Y.?
- Have you ever remodeled your home? Which rooms did you remodel? What did you do?
- Would you prefer to buy a new home or a fixer upper?
- Is it expensive to remodel a home?
- Do you prefer carpet or tile floors? Why?

Read about remodeling an old home.

Jay and Dawn Smith have just bought a house. The house is a fixer-upper so they got a good price on it. They looked at newer houses but could not find any they liked. The newer houses were also more expensive. Jay and Dawn are pretty handy around the house. They are able to do a lot of the work themselves. Some of the work they will hire out to a contractor. A contractor is a professional builder, carpenter, electrician, or plumber. Hiring a contractor can be expensive. The more work Jay and Dawn can do by themselves, the cheaper remodeling their new home will be. They are excited about creating their perfect home and making it just the way they want it.

The contractor will do the work that Jay and Dawn cannot do. He will re-wire the house and take down a wall. He will also put in new windows and doors. Dawn wanted a new kitchen counter and cabinets. The contractor will install those for the Smiths. Jay wants a big fireplace in the living room. He will have the contractor build it for him. Finally, the contractor will put in new pipes for the plumbing and install new toilets.

Jay and Dawn will do the rest of the remodeling themselves. They will lay new tile floors in the kitchen and bathroom. In the bedrooms, dining room, and living room they will lay carpeting. They will install new light fixtures in every room in the house. Jay will build shelves in the basement for storage. Eventually, they want to make the basement into rec room. Dawn wants to put in ceiling fans in the master bedroom and living room. The will have to paint all the rooms in the house. The Smith's know it will take a long time to finish remodeling their house. They think that it is worth it.

Would you like to buy this fixer-upper? Why?

Comprehension Questions:

1. Who just bought a house?
2. Was the house expensive? Why?
3. Why didn't Jay and Dawn buy a newer house?
4. What is a fixer-upper?
5. Are Jay and Dawn handy around the house?
6. Who will do the work that Jay and Dawn cannot do?
7. What will they do first?
8. Who will re-wire the house?
9. Who wants a new kitchen counter?
10. Will Jay install the new cabinets and doors?
11. Who will install the toilets?
12. Where will they put in tile floors?
13. What will they lay in the other rooms?
14. Where will they install new light fixtures?
15. Where will Jay build shelves?
16. What does Dawn want in the master bedroom?
17. Will they finish remodeling quickly?

Discussion Questions:

1. Have you ever bought a house? Was it new?
2. Are you handy around the house? What is the last thing you fixed in your house?
3. Do you know how to make something out of wood?
4. Do you think you would enjoy remodeling your home?
5. Do you have tile or carpeting in you home?
6. Do you live in an apartment or house? How long have you lived there?
7. Do you like newer homes or older homes? Why?
8. What is in the living room of your home?
9. Have you ever painted a room in your home?
10. Do most people in your country do remodeling work themselves or do they hire someone to do it for them?
11. Is it expensive to remodel in your country?
12. What kinds of things do people remodel?

Describe your ideal home.

- Where is it? What city and country is it in?
- How many floors does it have?
- How many rooms are there on each floor?
- What kind of furniture is in each room?
- Are there many plants?
- Is there a garden or a swimming pool?
- Is there a garage? How big is it?
- What other special things does your dream house have?

- Who usually cleans your house?
- Do you enjoy cleaning?
- What chores do you do?
- What is your least favorite household chore?
- Is housework only woman's work?
- Would you like to have a housekeeper? Why?
- What is spring-cleaning?
- Who takes out the garbage in your family? How often?

Read about housework.

Kelly is a 40-year-old woman. She is married and she has three kids. Jim, her husband, works all day at a bank. Kelly is a homemaker. She works hard everyday at home. She has many things to do. Some chores she does daily and some chores she does once or twice a week. In the morning, Kelly wakes the kids and makes breakfast for the family. Her husband takes them to school. After everyone leaves, she does the breakfast dishes and mops the kitchen floor. Then, it is time to do the laundry. She has to wash, dry, and fold the clothes. She also irons her husband's shirts.

Once a week, Kelly vacuums the house and dusts the furniture. Twice a week, she cleans the bathrooms. When her kids come home from school, Kelly helps them with their homework. Then, she makes dinner and sets the table. Her husband takes out the garbage after dinner. Jim has many chores to do as well. Every weekend he mows the lawn and pulls weeds in the garden. Sometimes he fixes things that are broken.

Kelly and Jim also have seasonal jobs. Every spring they do spring-cleaning. They wash all the windows in the house. They also clean out the garage. They get rid of things they don't want anymore. They plant flowers in the garden and seed the grass. In the fall, they rake the leaves. In the winter, they have to shovel the sidewalk when it snows. They don't have a snow blower. Kelly and Jim are very busy around the house. They are looking forward to their children growing up. Then, they will have some help doing all the cleaning, mowing, washing, dusting and vacuuming.

Comprehension Questions:

1. What is Kelly's husband's name?
2. How many kids do they have?
3. Does Kelly have job?
4. What does she do after breakfast?
5. What does she do with her husband's shirts?
6. How many times a week does she vacuum?
7. What does she dust?
8. How often does she clean the bathrooms?
9. Who helps the children with their homework?
10. Who takes out the garbage?
11. What does Jim do on weekends?
12. What do Kelly and Jim do in the spring?
13. What do they do in the fall?
14. What do they do in the winter?
15. Do they have a snow blower?

Discussion Questions:

1. Who usually cleans your home?
2. Do you like or dislike cleaning?
3. Who usually does the laundry in your family?
4. Who usually cooks the meals in your home?
5. Can you iron clothes? Do you ever iron your clothes?
6. Who does the dishes in your home?
7. Do you ever take the garbage out?
8. Do you ever recycle? Why?
9. What kinds of things are recyclable?
10. What chores do you do at home?
11. What chores did you do when you were a kid?
12. Have you ever mowed a lawn? Would you like to?
13. Have you ever shoveled snow? Would you like to?
14. Do you spring-clean? When? What do you do?
15. Is it okay for a man to do all the chores Kelly does?
16. Who usually cleans your bedroom? Is your bedroom messy or tidy right now?

Make a list of some chores and housework for your family to do.

Chore	Who	When

Lesson 21   Learning Foreign Languages

- Which are some popular languages for people to study?
- Why do people study foreign languages?
- What are some advantages of being bi-lingual?
- Students can do many things to improve their language-learning ability. How many can you think of? In your notebook make a list of things language students can do to improve their language ability.

Read about learning foreign languages.

People learn foreign languages for many different reasons. Students learn foreign language in school. Some students learn it because it is a required course that all students must take. Others learn a foreign language as an elective course. An elective course is a course that students choose to take. They choose electives that they are interested in or that they feel will be helpful to them in some way. Some people learn a foreign language for business reasons. They feel that learning a foreign language will be beneficial to their career or to their business. Other people learn foreign language for travel. They are going abroad and decide to learn the language of the country or countries that they will visit.

There are many different kinds of language learners. Some learners are fast and some are slow. Some like to study in a group, some like to study alone. Some learners think speaking is easy. Others think listening is easy. Some think reading is easy. Others think writing is easy. Some think that everything is easy. Others think that everything is very difficult. Some learners are confident, others are not confident. Some are outgoing, others are quiet and shy. Some like to keep a neat notebook, others like a messy notebook. Some students are always on time, others are often late. Some students do well on tests, others do poorly.

No matter what kind of student you are it is important to be prepared for class. This means you should have your book, pen, pencil, notebook, and dictionary. This way you will be prepared and will learn more than students who are not prepared. It is also important to review lessons after class. This way you can remember what you learned and not forget the new vocabulary, grammar and stories that you learned in the lesson.

Different students have different study habits. This means they differ in terms of where, when, how, and with whom they like to study. Some people like to study in the living room. Others like to study in the bedroom or study-room. Some study better in the morning or afternoon. Others study better in the evening or at night. Some people review often. Others like to learn as much new information as possible. Some students like to study with a friend or with a group of friends. Others like to study alone.

Different students like to study under different conditions. For example, some students prefer a bright room, others prefer a darker room. Some like to study with music or the TV in the background. Other students like to study in quiet. They think noses will disturb them when they study. This means that they cannot concentrate.

Comprehension Questions:

1. Why do people learn foreign languages?
2. What is a required course?
3. What is an elective course?
4. How are learners different in terms of speed?
5. How are learners different in terms of social environment?
6. What are the four basic skills of language learning?
7. How are learners different in terms of confidence?
8. How are learners different in terms of personality?
9. How are learners different in terms of punctuality?
10. How are learners different in terms of tests?
11. What does being 'prepared for class' mean?
12. Why is it important to be prepared for class?
13. Why is it important to review?
14. What different study habits do learners have?
15. Where do some learners like to study?
16. What different times of the day do learners like to study?
17. What different conditions do learners like?
18. What can disturb students?
19. How can this prevent them from successful studying?

Discussion questions:

1. How long have you learned English?
2. In what different places have you learned English?
3. Why are you learning English now?
4. Have you ever learned English or another language for other reasons?
5. What other languages are you interested in learning? Why?
6. Do you think learning a foreign language is easy or difficult? Why?
7. Which is easier for you: reading or writing? Listening or speaking?
8. What are your language-learning strong points? What are your language–learning weak points? How can you improve your weak points?
9. Do you like learning foreign languages? Why?
10. What other school subjects do you like? Why?
11. What school subjects do you dislike? Why?

12. Talk about your study habits:

   - Where do you usually study?
   - When do you usually study?
   - How do you usually study?
   - Who do you usually study with?
   - Do you usually study with bright lights?
   - Do you usually study in a noisy or quiet place?
   - What kinds of things can disturb you when you study?
   - How often do you study?

Lesson 22　Languages in Contemporary America

- What is the primary language in the USA? What other languages are there?
- What is the primary language in the your country? What other languages are there?
- America is a multi-lingual society. What does this mean?
- America is a multi-cultural-society. What does this mean?
- Is your country multi-lingual? Is your country multi-cultural?

Read about a recent change in American society.

Every ten years the US Census Bureau has a census. A census is a survey of the citizens in a country. The census shows different kinds of information about the population and how it changes or stays the same over the years. The Census Bureau sends questionnaires to every home in the country. A questionnaire is a list of questions for people to answer. When they finish answering the questions, people send the questionnaire back to the Census Bureau in Washington, D.C. where they analyze the results. This way, the government can get information about the country's citizens and their lives.

According to the 2000 census, nearly one in five Americans speaks a language other than English at home. This represents about 47 million people. This statistic is fifty percent higher than the last decade. According to the 1990 census, about one in seven people spoke a language other than English as their first language.

Spanish is the most popular language after English. 28.1 million people speak Spanish as their native language. Next is Chinese. 2 million people speak Chinese as their native language. Next is French (1.6 million), followed by German (1.4 million), and Tagalog, the native language of the Philippines, (1.2 million). Other languages include Korean, Vietnamese, Hindi, Native American languages and Russian.

People wonder about the reason for the increase in non-native speakers. The answer of course is more immigration to the USA. Between 1990 and 2000 there was a large increase in the number of immigrants to the USA. During this period Spanish-speaking population rose by 62 percent, and the Russian-speaking population tripled.

These population trends mean that the USA is becoming an increasingly multi-lingual and multi-cultural society. This will create a lot of challenges for many people, but ultimately it should make America a more interesting and colorful society.

Comprehension Questions:

1. How often does the US Census Bureau have a census?
2. What is a census?
3. What does a census show?
4. Where does the Census Bureau analyze the results?
5. Why do they analyze the results?
6. According the 2000 census, how many Americans speak a language other than English at home?
7. How many Americans spoke a language other than English at home in 1990?
8. Which language is the most popular after English?
9. How many people speak it?
10. Which language is next?
11. How many people speak it?
12. Which other languages are mentioned in the article?
13. What is the reason for the increase in non-native speakers?
14. How much did the Spanish-speaking population rise by?
15. How much did the Russian-speaking population increase?
16. What will these population trends cause?
17. What should America ultimately become?

Discussion Questions:

1. Why do you think some states have more non-native speakers than others?
2. What caused the increase in numbers of non-native speakers in the USA?
3. What kind of problems would non-native speakers have in the USA?

4. What languages are spoken in your country?
5. What kind of problems would people have in your country if they couldn't speak the local language? What could they do if they wanted to learn the local language?
6. How good is your English? Could you have a conversation with a native speaker? What would you talk about? What other languages would you like to learn? Why?

7. America is becoming a more multi-lingual society. What does this mean?
8. What kinds of challenges will this cause?
9. Say something positive about multi-lingual societies.
10. Say something negative about multi-lingual societies.
11. America also is an increasingly multi-cultural society. What does this mean?
12. What kinds of challenges will this cause?
13. Say something positive about multi-cultural societies.
14. Say something negative about multi-cultural societies.

15. What do you think about immigration?
16. What kinds of people immigrate to your country? How do you feel about them?
17. Would you like to immigrate? Why? Where?
18. Why do you think so many people want to immigrate to the USA?

Lesson 23   Life Story: Sam Harrison

- Are you grandparents still living?
- How old are your grandparents?
- Where did they come from?
- How big was their family?
- How many children did they have?
- What did they do for a living?
- Do you know any stories about your grandparents when they were young?

Read about Sam Harrison telling his life story.

My name is Sam Harrison and this is my life story. I am an American. I was born in 1937 in the state of Wisconsin. I grew up in a small town called Beloit with my parents and two younger brothers. I had a nice childhood. I went to Lincoln Elementary School. I played basketball and football in high school. My grades were pretty good. I had a girlfriend named Nancy. We dated for two years. We broke up after high school. I graduated from high school in 1955.

When I was 18 years old, I joined the United States Marines. I served on a ship in the South Pacific. I traveled to many different places like Singapore, Vietnam and Australia. While I was in the marines, I sometimes worked as a driver. Once I had to drive an important person to a dinner with some U.S. politicians. I did not know who the person was. I found out later it was the President of Vietnam. That was very exciting. After three years in the marines, I went to the University of Wisconsin. I was 21 years old and I didn't really like college. I had a few different sales jobs after college. In 1963, I got married, bought a house and settled in Chicago, Illinois.

We had five children and a cat named Kismet. I was an insurance salesman for 25 years. I didn't really like my job. We were not rich but I made a good living. I took long vacations with my family and enjoyed my life. In 1992, my wife and I got divorced. After the divorce, I quit my job and started working as a teacher. I taught children with learning problems. I also started writing children stories. In 1995, I had my first story published. I was very proud of that story. I moved to Phoenix, Arizona in 2002 with my new wife and our two dogs. I still teach and like to play golf. I really like Arizona and my kids visit me often.

Timeline: Sam's Life.

Think of some important events in Sam's life. Write them on the timeline.

| 1937 | 1940 | 1950 | 1960 | 1992 | 2002 | Present |

Comprehension Questions:

1. How old is Sam Harrison?
2. When was he born? Where was he born?
3. Which sports did he play in high school?
4. What was his girlfriend's name in high school?
5. When did he graduate from high school?
6. What did Sam do when he was eighteen years old?
7. Where did he travel to in the marines?
8. What did he sometimes do?
9. Which important person did he meet?
10. Which university did he go to?
11. What jobs did he do after college?
12. When did he get married?
13. Where did he and his wife live?
14. How many children did Sam and his wife have?
15. What was their cat's name?
16. Was he very rich?
17. When did he and his wife get divorced?
18. What did he do after the divorce?
19. What happened in 1995?
20. What did Sam do in 2002?
21. What does he do now?
22. Who often visits him?

Discussion Questions:

1. When were you born? Where were you born? Where did you grow up?
2. What high school did you go to? Did you enjoy it? How were your grades?
3. Did you play any sports in high school?
4. When you were a child, what did you want to be when you grew up?
5. What did your parents want you to be when you grew up?
6. Would you like to serve in the military? Why?
7. How many siblings do you have? Are they older or younger than you?
8. Do you get along with your siblings? How often do you see them?
9. Do you like to listen to your parents tell stories about when they were younger?
10. Did you go to college? How was it? What was your major?
11. What is something exciting that has happened in your life?

12. Have you ever been on a ship? Where did you go?
13. Do you know anyone who has gotten divorced?
14. Have you ever quit a job? Why did you quit?
15. How many different jobs have you had?
16. Do you have children? If so, how many? If not, do you want children?

17. Have you ever moved to a new house or city?
18. What are some positive things about moving to a new place?
19. What are some negative things about moving to a new place?
20. If you could move anywhere, where would you like to go? Why?

- Who is your favorite celebrity?
- What kinds of problems do celebrities have?
- Would you like to be a celebrity? Why?
- If you were going to be a celebrity, what would you like to be famous for?

Complete this sentence: ***I would like to be a famous*** _____

- What do you know about Muhammad Ali?
- What do you think of professional boxing? Is it an exciting sport?

Read about Muhammad Ali.

Muhammad Ali's nickname is 'The Greatest'. He was born Cassius Clay on January 17, 1942. He grew up in Louisville, Kentucky and started boxing when he was 12 years old. When he was 18, he boxed in the Olympic games and won a gold medal. He became a Muslim when he was 21. After the Olympics, he became a professional boxer. In 1964, he beat Sonny Liston and won the heavyweight title. He was only 22 years old. He describes his boxing style by saying, "I float like a butterfly and sting like a bee."

Muhammad Ali always worked to get equal rights for black Americans. In 1964, he changed his name from Cassius Clay to Muhammad Ali. He was against the U.S and Vietnam War because of his religion. He would not participate in the war so they took away his heavyweight title. Muhammad Ali did not fight again until 1970. He fought Joe Frazier in New York City and lost. Eventually, he won back the heavyweight title in 1974 when he beat George Foreman in Zaire, Africa.

In 1981, Muhammad Ali retired from boxing. He was diagnosed with Parkinson's disease in 1982. He made over US$50 million in his career. He wrote a book about his life in 1975 called "The Greatest: My Story". Muhammad Ali has been married four times. He has nine children and many grandchildren. He lit the torch at the 1996 Olympic games in Atlanta, Georgia. Today, Ali is still battling Parkinson's disease but he occasionally makes special appearances at fund-raisers.

Comprehension Questions:

1. Where was Muhammad Ali born?
2. What is his other name?
3. What is his religion?
4. What is his nickname?
5. When did he first win the heavyweight title?
6. How does he describe his fighting style?
7. Why was his title taken away?
8. How many times has he been married?
9. Where did he grow up?
10. When did he start boxing?
11. What did he win at the Olympics?
12. What was his original name?
13. Where did he fight George Foreman?
14. How many children does he have?
15. When did Ali retire?
16. What was he diagnosed with in 1982?
17. Where did he light the Olympic torch?
18. What does he do these days?

Discussion Questions:

1. Have you ever wanted to change your name? What did you want to change it to?
2. Do you think it is okay to change your name? Why?
3. Do you think everyone is equal? Do you or someone you know ever look down on other races or religions? Who? Why?
4. Did you ever have to fight or argue with people about something? Who? What?
5. What do you think of war? Are you against all wars? When do you think countries should go to war? Would you go to war if you were drafted?
6. If you were Muhammad Ali, would you have fought in the Vietnam War?

7. Do you like to watch the Olympics? Which events do you like to watch?
8. Does your country compete in the Olympics? Which sports do they compete in?
9. Have you ever thought about writing your life story? What would you call it?
10. Do you think anyone would want to buy a book about you? Why?

11. Who do you feel had a more interesting life: Sam Harrison or Muhammad Ali? Who do you think had a harder life? Why?
12. Whose life would you rather live: Sam Harrison's, Muhammad Ali's, or your own?
13. Would you like to be famous or stay 'unknown and ordinary'? Why?
14. What would you like to be famous for?
15. What problems do celebrities face? Is being famous worth it?
16. What sad celebrity stories do you know about?

17. Who are some famous people from your country? Why are they famous? Try to think of people from these different fields:
entertainment / government / history / sports / business / education military / literature / food.

Matchmaker: 1

- Where can two people go on a romantic date?
- Where can people go to meet other people?
- How do you decide if you like someone?
- How do you decide if you don't like someone?

Read the following situation.

You and your sweetheart are very happy together. You have similar tastes in many things and there are many things that you like to do together. For example, you both enjoy going out to eat. You also both like Italian food, so you often go out to Italian restaurants together. You also both like to listen to music. So you often stay home and listen to a CD. There are many things you like to do together. You wish everyone was as happy as you are. This makes you think about your friends who are single and don't have a sweetheart right now. You and your sweetheart can think of eight people you both know who are single. Luckily there are four males and four females. You and your sweetheart decide to play matchmaker. This means you want to introduce your friends to each other. You hope that they will be interested in each other and that romance will begin. Then everyone could be as happy as you are with your sweetheart.

Comprehension Questions:

1. Why are you and your sweetheart so happy?
2. What do you like to do together?
3. What do you wish?
4. How many single people do you and your sweetheart know?
5. What do you decide to do?
6. What does this mean?
7. What do you hope?
8. How happy do you hope your friends will be?

Read about your eight single friends.

Name	Brian	Chris	Michael	Robert
Job	High school teacher	Car mechanic	Law student	Nurse
Appearance	Medium height A little overweight	Tall, Slim	Medium height. Medium build	Short. A little overweight
Personality	Serious, smart	Shy, quiet	Outgoing, funny	Kind, gentle
Interests	Sports, hiking	Movies, cars	Novels, art	Cooking, music
Wants	To meet an active girl	To have a good time	To have a good conversation	A quiet night at home

Name	Elizabeth	Julia	Susan	Veronica
Job	Doctor	Art student	Kindergarten teacher	Secretary
Appearance	Short. A little overweight	Medium height. Medium build	Tall. Slim	Medium height. Overweight
Personality	Kind, gentle	Shy, quiet	Serious, smart	Outgoing, funny
Interests	Movies, art	Taking walks	Restaurants	Shopping, driving
Wants	To see a good movie	To do something outdoors	To meet a smart guy	To enjoy herself

Discussion Questions:

1. Your job is to be a matchmaker for these eight people. Try to make four good couples. Consider each person's job, appearance, personality, and interests. Try to find four good couples of two suitable people. Write the four couples in the chart:

```
1. _____ and _____     2. _____ and _____



3. _____ and _____     4. _____ and _____
```

2. Who did you match with whom? Explain your choices to your classmates.

3. Where could these four couples go on a date? Think of some interesting places for them to go. What can they do at these places?

4. What kind of personality do you like for a friend?
5. What kind of personality do you like romantically?
6. What kind of appearance do you like for a friend?
7. What kind of appearance do you like romantically?
8. What is more important for a romantic relationship, appearance or personality?
9. What is more important for a friendship, appearance or personality?

10. Describe your appearance.
11. Describe your personality.

12. After a few years together, romance sometimes begins to fade? What causes this?
13. How can a couple keep their relationship romantic if romance starts to fade?

Read the following situation.

You and your spouse have two children. You have a 28-year old daughter and a 32 year-old son. They both have good jobs: your daughter is an advertising designer and your son is an engineer. Your daughter enjoys outdoor activities and art. Your son likes to go fishing to or to the park. They are both quite successful, but don't really have time to meet anyone romantically. Also, they are both a little shy and introverted, so it is not always easy for them to meet new people. You and your spouse have decided to help them. You go to a dating agency and tell them your situation. The dating agency calls you and gives you details about eight single people who they think could be compatible with your daughter and with your son.

Read about the four male choices for your daughter.

Name	Barry	Kevin	Norman	Paul
Occupation	High School Math Teacher	Salesman	Lawyer	Doctor
Appearance	Tall, slim	Medium height, medium build	Short, a little overweight	Medium height, a little overweight
Personality	Kind, friendly	Outgoing, funny	Shy, smart	Serious, quiet
Hobbies	Sports, health	Music, art	Movies, novels	Hiking, camping
Age	28	36	32	44

Read about the four female choices for your son.

Name	Christine	Melanie	Sarah	Violet
Occupation	Nurse	Artist	Boutique Clerk	Fashion Designer
Appearance	Short, a little overweight	Medium height, medium build	Tall, slim	Medium height, overweight
Personality	Kind, funny	Shy, intelligent	Serious, smart	Outgoing, active
Hobbies	Visiting friends, seeing movies	Reading, gardening	Travel, fitness	Architecture, cooking
Age	36	32	28	30

Comprehension Questions:

1. How many children do you and your spouse have?
2. What kind of work do they do?
3. What do they enjoy doing?
4. What is their problem?
5. How do you and your spouse help them?
6. How many candidates does the agency select?
7. What are the males' names?
8. What are their occupations?
9. What are their appearances like?
10. What are their personalities like?
11. What are their hobbies?
12. What are their ages?
13. What are the females' names?
14. What are their occupations?
15. What are their appearances like?
16. What are their personalities like?
17. What are their hobbies?
18. What are their ages?

Fill in your own personal information:

Name

Occupation

Appearance

Personality

Hobbies

Age

Discussion Questions:

1. Which male candidate do you feel is most suitable for the daughter in this situation? Why did you choose this one?
2. Which male candidate do you feel is least suitable for the daughter in this situation? Why did you choose this one?
3. Which female candidate do you feel is most suitable for the son in this situation? Why did you choose this one?
4. Which female candidate do you feel is least suitable for the son in this situation? Why did you choose this one?

- Pretend you have to choose one of these people as a friend for yourself.

    5. Which of the male candidates do you like best? Why?
    6. Which of the female candidates do you like best? Why?
    7. Which of the male candidates do you like least? Why?
    8. Which of the female candidates do you like least? Why?

9. Which characteristic do you think is most important for a romantic partner: Occupation, Appearance, Personality, Hobbies or Age? Why?
10. Which characteristic do you think is least important for a romantic partner: Occupation, Appearance, Personality, Hobbies or Age? Why?

11. Which characteristic do you think is most important in a friend: Occupation, Appearance, Personality, Hobbies or Age? Why?
12. Which characteristic do you think is least important in a friend: Occupation, Appearance, Personality, Hobbies or Age? Why?

Lesson 27   Going to a Rock Concert

- Have you ever been to a live concert?
- What kinds of concerts do you like to go to?
- Do you think rock concerts are exciting? Why?
- What kind of music do you like to listen to?
- When do you usually listen to music?
- Where do you usually listen to music?
- Why do you usually listen to music?

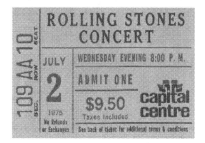

Read about going to a rock concert.

Bob and Tim enjoy going to rock concerts. They like seeing their favorite bands. Bob's favorite bands are Radiohead and Oasis. Tim likes the Irish band U2 and the White Stripes. They both like classic rock bands such as the Beatles, Rolling Stones and Led Zeppelin. They love Elvis Presley. They have seen many rock concerts. They have seen concerts in big stadiums with 30,000 seats. They have seen concerts in theaters that only seat 4,000. They usually wait in line many hours to buy concert tickets.

Last night, Bob and Tim saw the rock band Pearl Jam. The band was playing at the Midway Theater, which has 5,000 seats. Bob and Tim won two front row seats to the concert. They also won two backstage passes. The concert was scheduled to start at 9:00 pm. Bob and Tim wore blue jeans and t-shirts. The band did not start playing until 9:20. They were really loud. There was a drummer, two electric guitarists, a bass guitarist and the lead singer. They all had long hair. Some wore leather pants and others torn jeans. They played many songs. Some were from their new CD and some were from their old CDs. Pearl Jam wrote all the songs.

The band finished playing and left the stage. The audience kept cheering for an encore. The band came back on stage. They played two more songs. Bob and Tim thought it was a great show. Tim caught a guitar pick that one of the guitarists threw. Both Bob's and Tim's ears were ringing. Bob bought a Pearl Jam concert t-shirt. They went backstage and got autographs from the band. Later, they went to the pub and told their friends about the show. They all thought the concert was very exciting.

Comprehension Questions:

1. Where do Bob and Tim like to go?
2. Who are Tim's favorite bands?
3. Who are Bob's favorite bands?
4. Who are some classic rock bands?
5. What band did Bob and Tim see last night?
6. How do Bob and Tim usually get tickets?
7. How did they get tickets for Pearl Jam?
8. What did they wear to the concert?
9. What time did the band start playing?
10. What instruments did the band play?
11. What did the band look like?
12. Who wrote the songs Pearl Jam played?
13. What is an encore?
14. What did Tim catch?
15. What is a backstage pass?
16. What did Bob buy?

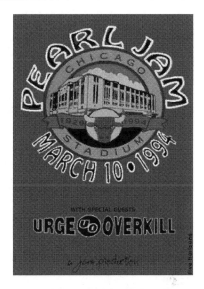

Discussion Questions:

1. Have you ever been to a rock concert?
2. Do you think rock concerts are too loud?
3. Do you like rock music? What kinds of music do you like?
4. Who are your favorite bands or singers?
5. Have you ever heard of The Beatles? The Rolling Stones? Pearl Jam?

6. How long would you stand in line for tickets? Would you stay overnight?
7. How do you feel about piercing? Do you have anything pierced?
8. What do you think of men with long hair?
9. What do you think of men with tattoos?
10. What do you think of women with short hair?
11. What do you think of women with tattoos?
12. If you were going to get a tattoo, what would it be?

13. Would you ask a famous person for their autograph if you saw them on the street?
14. Is there a time when you shouldn't ask someone for his or her autograph? When?
15. Did you ever want to be a rock star? Did you ever want to be famous?
16. Rock concerts can be loud. Would you like to go to a loud rock concert?
17. Have your ears ever rung because of loud noise? Why? How long did they ring?
18. How old should someone be to be able to go to a rock concert without an adult?

19. What kinds of music CDs do you buy? What are some of your favorites?
20. What was the last music CD you bought? Why did you buy this one?
21. Do you ever download music from the Internet? What kinds?
22. What other things do people download from the Internet?

Lesson 28   Music: A Symphony

- Do you like classical music?
- Who are some famous composers?
- What instruments do musicians play in orchestras?
- Which instrument is your favorite?
- Can you play a musical instrument?
- Which instrument would you like to learn? Why?
- Would you like to go to a symphony orchestra concert? Why?
- If you went to a symphony concert what would you wear? Why?

Read about going to a symphony orchestra concert.

An orchestra is a musical group used most often in classical music. Full size orchestras are called symphony orchestras. Jay and Dawn enjoy going to the symphony. They are season ticket holders for the Boston Symphony Orchestra. The Boston Symphony Orchestra plays their concerts at Symphony Hall. Jay and Dawn both love classical music. Jay's favorite composers are Beethoven, Stravinsky and Tchaikovsky. Dawn's favorite composers are Mozart, Bach and Rachmaninoff. The Boston Symphony plays music from many different composers. They do not write their own music.

Jay and Dawn went to a symphony orchestra concert last Saturday night. The performance started at 8:00 pm. Jay and Dawn went out for dinner before the concert. Jay wore a suit and tie and Dawn wore a nice dress. The usher gave them a program after he seated them. The orchestra started on time. The conductor wore a black tuxedo with tails. All the musicians wore dressy black clothes. First, they played a violin concerto by Mozart. Then, they had a fifteen-minute intermission. They flashed the lights when the orchestra was ready to start again. The orchestra came back and played Beethoven's 3rd Symphony.

There were many different musicians in the symphony. They all played different kinds of instruments. A typical symphony orchestra usually consists of four groups or sections of musical instruments:

- The strings (violins, violas, cellos, double basses),
- The woodwinds (flutes, clarinets, oboes, bassoons),
- The brass (trumpets, trombones, tuba, french horns), and
- The percussion (timpani, snare drum, bass drum, cymbals, etc.).

When the orchestra finished, the audience clapped. The conductor turned around and bowed to the audience. After the show, Jay and Dawn went to a café. They had some wine. Jay had a piece of strawberry cheesecake. Dawn had a slice of key lime pie. They talked about the music they had heard that evening and discussed their favorite parts of the performance. They both enjoyed the concert very much. Dawn liked the symphony best. Jay preferred the concerto.

55

Comprehension Questions:

1. What is an orchestra?
2. What is a symphony orchestra?
3. What do Jay and Dawn both love?
4. Which composers are Jay's favorites?
5. Which composers are Dawn's favorites?
6. When did they go to a symphony orchestra?
7. What did they wear?
8. What did the conductor wear?
9. What did the musicians wear?
10. What did they play first?
11. What happened after the intermission?
12. How many groups of instruments are in a typical symphony?
13. What instruments are in the string section?
14. What instruments are in the woodwinds section?
15. What instruments are in the brass section?
16. What instruments are in the percussion section?
17. What did Jay and Dawn do after the show?
18. What did Jay have?
19. What did Dawn have?
20. Which part of the show did Dawn like best?
21. Which part of the show did Jay prefer?

Discussion Questions:

1. How many CDs do you have?
2. What kinds of CDs do you have?
3. Do you ever download music from the Internet?
4. Do you think sharing music through the Internet is okay?
5. Can you play a musical instrument? If so, what do you play? Can you play well?
6. Which instruments are your favorites? Why?
7. Which instruments do you think are easy to learn? Which ones are more difficult?
8. Do you think it is important for children to learn how to play an instrument? Why?
9. Do you enjoy watching music videos on TV? Why?
10. Do you like all kinds of music?

11. What is your favorite kind of music?
12. What kind of music do you dislike? Why do you dislike it?
13. Would you like to have an expensive stereo system? Why?
14. Is music an important part of your life? Why?
15. Can you sing well? Do you have a nice voice?
16. What songs do you like to sing?
17. Do you like to sing karaoke? Why?
18. How do you feel about performing in front of an audience?
19. Do you often listen to music on the radio?
20. What is your favorite radio station? Why do you like this one?

- Where can you learn about current events?
- Do you prefer to get news from the newspaper or radio?
- Do you watch TV news? Which channel do you usually watch? Why do you watch this channel?
- Do you ever get news from the Internet?
- Which kind of news is most important or interesting to you: local, national, or international news?
- What is the difference between news and gossip?

Read these news reports about current events.

- There were numerous tornadoes yesterday in the state of Texas. They touched down near Dallas and destroyed hundreds of homes. They also destroyed a local elementary school. Firefighters are trying to put out fires caused by the tornadoes. Texas Governor Bob Hammond has called in the National Guard for help. Thousands of people are without electricity.

- In local news, the Stop-and-Go mini-mart on Maple Street was robbed last night. Police say two men with guns wearing black ski masks entered the store around 11:30 pm. They took $700 and some food items. The clerk and one customer were in the store at the time of the robbery. Police are looking for a dark blue van with Florida license plates.

- On the lighter side, Marine Park has added a new attraction. Sparky the dolphin just arrived yesterday afternoon to a big welcome. Sparky was flown over from Marine Park in California to his new home here in Miami. Sparky is two years old and quite friendly. People will be able to see Sparky perform next month in the new dolphin water show.

- Finally, the sports. In baseball, the Seattle Mariners played the Chicago White Sox at Comiskey Park in Chicago. The Mariners beat the White Sox 4 to 1. Seattle's pitcher, Jim Gibson, pitched 8 innings. Seattle's first baseman, Steve Mercer, hit a grand slam homerun. White Sox catcher, Joe Patterson, was hit by a pitch.

Comprehension Questions:

1. What happened in Texas?
2. What was destroyed?
3. How many people are without electricity?
4. What are the firefighters doing?
5. What is the governor's name?
6. What did he do?
7. What store was robbed?
8. What street is the mini-mart on?
9. How much did the robbers take?

10. Who was in the store at the time of the robbery?
11. What were the robbers wearing?
12. What are police looking for?
13. When did Sparky arrive at Marine Park?
14. What kind of animal is Sparky?
15. Where did Sparky come from? How did he get to Miami?
16. How old is Sparky?
17. When will people be able to see him perform?
18. What two teams played each other?
19. What sport do they play?
20. Where did they play?
21. Who pitched for Seattle?
22. Who hit a Grand Slam?
23. What happened to the White Sox catcher?

Discussion Questions:

1. Are you interested in disaster stories such as earthquakes and tornadoes? Why?
2. Are you interested in more good new or bad news? Why?
3. Has your home ever been damaged by a typhoon or earthquake? What was damaged? Was it expensive to repair?
4. How can you prepare your home for a typhoon or an earthquake?
5. How do you feel when you see stories about crime? Do they frighten you?
6. Do you like feel-good stories? Do you think they are boring?
7. Do you like news about sports? Do you keep up with your local sports teams?
8. What are some current local news stories you find interesting?
9. What are some current world news stories you find interesting?
10. What are some current national news stories you find interesting?
11. What is your favorite news channel? Who is the anchorman or anchorwoman?
12. Which story from the text do you find the most interesting? Why?
13. What newspaper do you read? Why?

Make a list of some recent current events stories. Try to think of some local, national, and international stories. Write them in the chart.

Local Stories	National Stories	International Stories

Lesson 30   Gossip

- Do you ever gossip? With whom? About what?
- Do you like to gossip? Why or why not?
- What do you and your friends usually talk about?
- Who are your favorite celebrities?
- Do you read about your favorite stars personal lives?
- Do you have any good gossip you can share?

Read these celebrity gossip reports.

Blonde babe Britney continues to deny rumors she is having an affair with TV hunk Joey Long. The two have been seen having dinner together and holding hands. Joey Long, who stars on the hit TV show "Teen Years", has neither denied nor confirmed the rumors. A spokesperson for Britney said, "They do not have a romantic relationship. Britney and Joey are just "good friends" and they like to spend time together." Britney is scheduled to attend the Pop Music Awards show next week. She has not said who her date will be, but I think we can guess who it will be.

Eddie James, lead guitarist for the rock band Final Days, has been arrested for disturbing the peace and resisting arrest. According to reports, police were called to Eddie James' house last night because of loud noise. Mr. James started shouting at the police and throwing bottles. Police arrested him and took him to the police station. He was released this morning. He faces a possible $2000 fine and 30 days in jail if convicted. He has been arrested twice before for the same offense.

In movie news, a woman from Denver, Colorado is suing actor George Clancy. The woman claims she met the popular actor while he was filming a movie near Denver. The woman says they had a month long affair and later she became pregnant. George Clancy says he met the woman but they never had an affair. Clancy has been married to his wife, Sally, for ten years. They have two teenage daughters and a three-year-old son. The woman plans to sue Clancy for child support.

Comprehension Questions:

1. Where have Britney and Joey been seen?
2. What were they doing?
3. What's the name of Joey Long's TV show?
4. What color is Britney's hair?
5. Has Joey confirmed the rumors?
6. Who said they do not have a romantic relationship?
7. Where is Britney going next week?
8. What's the name of Eddie James' band?
9. What kind of music do they play?
10. What did he get arrested for?
11. Where did he get arrested?
12. When was he released?
13. How much might he have to pay?
14. Has he been arrested before? On what charges?
15. What does George Clancy do for a living?
16. Who is suing him?
17. What happened to the woman after the month long affair?
18. How long has George Clancy been married?
19. Does he have any children?

Discussion Questions:

1. Do you like to gossip? What do you like to gossip about?
2. Do you think gossip can hurt people?
3. Do you like it when people gossip about you?
4. Have you ever been hurt by gossip? How?
5. Do your friends like gossiping?
6. What do you and your friends like to talk about?
7. Do you know anyone who has been hurt by gossip? What happened?
8. What do people gossip about in your country?
9. Is there anything you shouldn't gossip about?

10. Are you a trustworthy person? Can people trust you?
11. What was the last secret that someone told you? Did you keep it or break it?
12. Do you usually trust people to keep a secret?
13. Who do you trust the most in your life right now? Who do you not trust? Why?
14. Why do people gossip? What do people often gossip about?
15. What kind of gossip do you usually hear? Do you usually believe it?
16. Do you ever tell stories about people even if you are not sure they are true?
17. Sometimes we tell people, "Mind your own business". What does this mean?

18. Which newspapers do you read? Do you like to read about celebrities?
19. Who are the paparazzi? What do they do? How do you feel about them?
20. Did you ever secretly take pictures of people? Who? Where? Why?
21. Are you interested in pictures of celebrities in their private lives? Why?
22. Which celebrities are often in the news these days? Do you like them? Why?

Ordering From the Menu

- What do you usually have for breakfast?
- Where do you usually have breakfast?
- What do you usually have for lunch?
- Where do you usually have lunch?
- Look at these menus for breakfast and lunch. Read the items and prices. Which choices look good to you?

Breakfast Menu

Main Course:

2 Eggs with ham, bacon, or sausage.......	3.50
3 Eggs with ham, bacon, or sausage.......	4. 50
Plain omelet with toast...........................	2.75
Cheese omelet with toast.....................	3.25
Ham omelet with toast...........................	3.50
Ham and cheese omelet with toast............	4.00
2 Pancakes with maple syrup..................	3.00
3 Pancakes with maple syrup..................	4. 25
Cereal with fruit and toast	2.75

Side Dishes:

Ham, bacon or sausage	1.25
1 Egg	1.00
Toast	1.00
Pancake	1.50
Fruit	seasonal

Beverages:

Orange juice or tomato juice..........	1.00
Coffee or tea	0.75
Milk / regular or chocolate	1.00

Lunch Menu

Main Course:

Tuna sandwich with soup	4.00
Steak sandwich with soup	5.50
Meatball sandwich with soup	4. 75
Fried chicken with salad	6.00
Pizza with salad	5.50
Hamburger with French fries	4.00
Hot dog with French fries	3.75
Spaghetti with garlic bread	5.00
Lasagna with garlic bread	6.00

Side Dishes:

Bowl of soup	1.75
Salad	1.75
French fries	1.50
Onion rings	1.50
Garlic bread	1.00
Garlic bread with cheese	2.00

Beverages:

Soda	1.00
Mineral water	1.00
Juice	1.75
Ice tea / ice coffee	1.50

Comprehension Questions:

1. How many breakfast main courses are there?
2. How many breakfast side dishes are there?
3. How many breakfast beverages are there?
4. Which main course is the most expensive?
5. Which main course is the cheapest?
6. Which side dish is the most expensive?
7. Which side dish is the cheapest?
8. Which beverage is the most expensive?
9. Which beverage is the cheapest?

10. How many lunch main courses are there?
11. How many lunch side dishes are there?
12. How many lunch beverages are there?
13. Which main course is the most expensive?
14. Which main course is the cheapest?
15. Which side dish is the most expensive?
16. Which side dish is the cheapest?
17. Which beverage is the most expensive?
18. Which beverage is the cheapest?

Discussion Questions:

1. Which breakfast main course would you like?
2. Which breakfast side dish would you like?
3. Which breakfast beverage would you like?
4. Repeat your breakfast order:

• *I would like _____ with _____ on the side and _____ to drink for breakfast.*

5. What is the total cost of your breakfast order?
   Add 8 percent tax and 15 percent tip.
6. Which lunch main course would you like?
7. Which lunch side dish would you like?
8. Which lunch beverage would you like?
9. Repeat your lunch order:

• *I would like _____ with _____ on the side and _____ to drink for lunch.*

10. What is the total cost of your lunch order?
    Add 8 percent tax and 15 percent tip.
11. Would you like to go to this restaurant for breakfast? Why?
12. Would you like to go to this restaurant for lunch? Why?
13. What would you rather have for lunch that is not on this menu?
14. Do you prefer to have breakfast at home or out? Why?
15. Do you prefer to have lunch at home or out? Why?
16. Do you ever make breakfast at home? What do you make?
17. Do you ever make lunch? What do you make?

- What do you like to eat?
- What don't you like to eat?
- What do you like to talk about?
- What don't you like to talk about?
- Who do you usually have dinner with? What do you talk about?
- Where do you usually have dinner? What do you usually have?

Read the following situation.

You and your spouse are going to have a dinner party for some of your friends. However, you have one problem: you don't really know each other's friends very well. This is the main reason you want to have a dinner party. This way you can get to know each other's friends better and your friends can get to know each other as well. You both feel that this is an important thing for a good marriage. You feel that it is important to know each other's friends.

Each of you decides to invite four friends to the dinner party. This will make a total of ten people: you, your spouse, four of your friends and four of your spouse's friends. For the dinner party, there are two main things to consider. The first is what to serve for dinner. Each of your friends has different things that they like and don't like to eat. You want to be sure that everyone is satisfied with his or her meal. The second is where to seat everyone. Each of your friends has different things that they like and don't like to talk about. You want to be sure that everyone is satisfied with his or her dinner conversation.

So, you and your spouse need to consider these two things: what to serve for dinner, and where everyone should be seated, so they can have a good conversation with the person seated next to them.

Comprehension Questions:

1. What kind of party are you going to have?
2. What is the problem?
3. What do you feel is important for a good marriage?
4. Who do you feel it is important to know?
5. How many friends will each of you invite?
6. How many people will be at the party in total?
7. How many main things are there to consider?
8. What is the first thing to consider?
9. What do your friends like to eat?
10. What do you want to be sure?
11. What is the second thing to consider?
12. What do your friends like to talk about?
13. What do you want to be sure?
14. What are the two points to consider again?

Read what everyone likes to eat and talk about.

Person:	Food:	Conversation Interests:
You	Steak, seafood	Anything
Your spouse	Seafood, salad	Anything
Bob	Shrimp, pasta	Business, sports
Bill	Steak, potatoes	Sports, stock market
Karen	Steak, pasta	Exercise, gardening
Kate	Seafood, salad	Music, movies
Duncan	Chicken, potatoes	Business, cooking
Dennis	Seafood, rice	Sports, movies
Barbara	Chicken, rice	Sports, books
Brenda	Seafood, pasta	Cooking, stock market

Discussion Questions:

1. What could you serve for appetizers? Choose two. Why did you choose these?
2. What kind of soup could you serve? Choose one. Why did you choose this?
3. What main courses could you serve? Choose two. Why did you choose these?
4. What side dishes could you serve? Choose three. Why did you choose these?
5. You will have dinner at a round table. This means that each person has two neighbors with whom they must have conversations. In the space below draw a seating chart for your dinner party. Write down where each person will sit.

Lesson 33   The Exchange Students

- What is an exchange student?
- Imagine if you were an exchange student:

1. Where would you like to go?
2. What would you like to study?
3. When would you prefer to go?
4. What problems would you likely have?
5. What would you probably miss about your home and your home country?

Read about two language students.

Frank is an American student. He studies Japanese at UCLA in California. He has studied Japanese for two years. In the first semester of their junior year, UCLA language students can go abroad to study. They have a student exchange program with various universities in various cities in various countries all over the world. They have exchange programs with Tokyo University and Osaka University in Japan. Junior year, Japanese language students go to either one of these universities for one semester. While they are there they learn many things. They learn language at the university and they also learn Japanese history, art and religion. They can learn about many aspects of Japanese culture. The language students stay with a Japanese family while they are in Japan. This way they can learn about Japanese society. They can spend time with a family and get to know them. They can learn about how Japanese family members communicate and interact with each other. This kind of experience is very valuable for language learning. To learn a language well and fluently, it helps to spend some time in an environment where the language is spoken. For Japanese-language students this means they should spend some time in Japan.

Tanaka is a Japanese student. He studies English literature at Tokyo University in Japan. He has studied English literature for four years and English language for ten years. In the first semester of their junior year, English language students can go abroad to study. They have a student exchange program with various universities in various cities in various countries all over the world. They have exchange programs with universities in the USA, Canada, the U K, Australia, New Zealand and South Africa. Junior year English language students go to either one of these countries for one semester. While they are there they learn many things. They learn language at the university and they also learn the history, art and religion of the country in which they are studying. They can learn about many aspects of Western culture. The language students stay with a Western family while they are abroad. This way they can learn about Western society. They can spend time with a family and get to know them. They can learn about how Western family members communicate and interact with each other. This kind of experience is very valuable for language learning. To learn a language well and fluently, it helps to spend some time in an environment where the language is spoken. For English-language students this means they should spend some time in one of the English-speaking countries of the world.

Comprehension Questions:

1. Where does Frank study? What is his major?
2. Where can UCLA Japanese language students go abroad to study?
3. What things can they learn at university?
4. Who can they stay with? What can they learn there?
5. What should Japanese language students do? Why?
6. Where does Tanaka study? What is his major?
7. Where can Tokyo University English language students go abroad to study?
8. What things can they learn at university?
9. Who can they stay with? What can they learn there?
10. What should English language students do? Why?

Discussion Questions:

1. If you went to another country what things would be different there?
2. How are Americans different from people in your country?
3. How are Japanese different from people in your country?
4. If you were an exchange student would you rather go to the USA or to Japan? Why?
5. Why do language students participate in student exchanges?
6. Do you think student exchange programs are a good idea? Why?

7. Think of some differences between different English speaking countries.
   How are the USA and the U K different? How are Canada and Australia different?
   How are South Africa and New Zealand different?
8. How are these countries similar to each other?

9. Culture comparison. Choose two countries with which you are quite familiar.
   Compare and contrast things in their cultures. Fill in the chart.

Country:		
Location:		
Size:		
People:		
Religion:		
Climate:		
Language:		
Food:		
History:		
Currency:		
Cost:		
Famous places and landmarks:		
Famous people:		

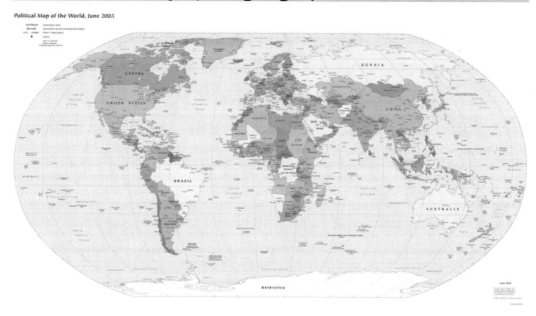

Political Map of the World, June 2003

- Look at the World Map. Can you find these different countries?
- Fill in the chart with the appropriate nationality and language for each country.

Country	Nationality	Language
1. Australia		
2. China		
3. England		
4. Germany		
5. Greece		
6. Holland		
7. India		
8. Italy		
9. Japan		
10. South Korea		
11. Portugal		
12. Thailand		
13. The USA		
14. Vietnam		

Comprehension Questions:

1. Chris is from Australia. What language does he speak?
2. Chen Lei is Chinese. What language does he speak?
3. What language do people speak in England?
4. What nationality speaks German?
5. Nikolas is from Greece. What language does he speak?
6. What language do people speak in Holland?
7. Ashok is Indian. What country is he from?
8. What nationality is someone from Italy?
9. Miko is from Japan. What language does she speak?
10. What language do people from Korea speak?
11. What nationality is someone from Portugal?
12. What language do people from Thailand speak?
13. John is from The USA. What's his nationality?
14. What language do people from Vietnam speak?

Discussion Questions:

1. Do you know where all these countries are? Say something about each of the fifteen countries from above. Talk about the country's geography or culture.
2. Try to name a city in each of the countries.
3. What kind of food do you think people eat in the different countries?
4. Would you like to eat this kind of food?
5. Do you like to travel? Why?
6. Which of these countries would you like to visit? Why?
7. Which of these countries would you not want to visit? Why?
8. Would you rather go to Australia or China? Why?
9. Would you rather go to England or Germany? Why?
10. Would you rather go to Greece or Holland? Why?
11. Would you rather go to Japan or Korea? Why?
12. Would you rather go to the USA or India? Why?
13. Try to find each country's flag.

Fears and Phobias

- What things are you afraid of?
- Do you know anyone who is afraid of heights?
- What is the difference between a fear and a phobia?
- What do you do when you are scared?
- Talk about a time when you were really scared.

Read about phobias.

It is normal for people to be afraid of things like snakes, spiders, or the dark. A phobia is an irrational or unreasonable fear. Phobias are different because they are an extremely strong fear of a situation or thing. They are also a kind of fear that doesn't go away. A person who has a phobia will be afraid of something every time he or she sees or experiences it. They won't just be afraid once or twice. People who have phobias often go out of their way to avoid the situation or thing that scares them.

Sometimes when a phobic is forced to face what makes them scared, they may get very nervous and have a panic attack. This can make them feel even more anxious and upset. Panic attacks can be really scary. They may make a person shake, sweat, and breathe quickly. Some people who have a panic attack experience chest pains, dizziness, loss of breath, or an accelerated heart rate. A panic attack can cause someone to think something awful is going to happen and that they are losing control. Some people who have panic attacks say that when the attacks are happening, they feel like they can't think straight or that they're "going crazy."

Panic attacks only last a short time, but to someone who is having one, they feel much longer. Sometimes, even if a person knows that their phobia doesn't make sense, they may not be able to stop their mind and body from reacting and having a panic attack.

Phobia	Fear of...
Claustrophobia	confined spaces
Dentophobia	dentists
Xenophobia	strangers or foreigners
Glossophobia	speaking in public
Testophobia	taking tests
Homophobia	homosexuality
Acrophobia	heights
Agoraphobia	open spaces or crowded places

Comprehension Questions:

1. Is it normal to be afraid of things?
2. How is a phobia different from a fear?
3. Does a phobia go away?
4. What do people with phobias go out of their way to do?
5. How can a panic attack make someone feel?
6. What can a panic attack make someone do?
7. Does a person having a panic attack feel in control'?
8. How long do panic attacks last?
9. Can a person stop a panic attack from happening?
10. What is agoraphobia?
11. What is the fear of confined spaces called?
12. What is the fear of dentists called?
13. What is the fear of speaking in public called?
14. What is homophobia?
15. What is the fear of heights called?

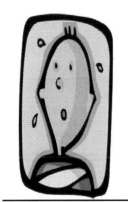

Discussion Questions:

1. What were you afraid of when you were a child?
2. What are you afraid of now? Why are you afraid of these things?
3. Are you afraid of any people? Who? Why are you afraid of them?
4. Talk about a time when you were really scared. What were you afraid of? What did it feel like? What happened? What did you do? Are you still afraid of this?

5. Make a list of some things that scare you. Compare your list with a classmate's list. How can you try to overcome these fears?

6. What things make you nervous? Talk about a time when you were very nervous.
7. What is the difference between being scared and being nervous?
8. If you are feeling nervous or scared how do you make yourself relax?
9. Imagine you are home alone late at night. Are you scared? Of what?

10. Read the following paragraph.

"My heart starts beating so fast . . . it feels like it's going to explode. My throat closes and I can't breathe. I start to choke. My hands start sweating. I get so dizzy I have to hold onto the furniture or the wall to keep from falling or fainting. I know I'm going to die. I want to run, but I don't know where."

- What is this an example of?
- Have you ever felt this way?
- What should this person do?

11. What kinds of treatments are there for phobias?
12. If you had a phobia would you want to get help? Why?
13. What other phobias do people sometimes have?

Lesson 36   Problems, Advice, and Suggestions

- What personal problems do you have right now?
- What problems have you had in the past?
- Have you ever asked anyone for advice about your personal problems? Who did you ask? What did they suggest?
- Has anyone ever asked you for advice about a personal problem?
- What was their problem? What did you suggest?

Read about eight people and their personal problems.

1. John can't sleep at night. He has tried to go to bed earlier and wake up earlier, but he can't. He often has trouble sleeping at night. When he finally can sleep, it is usually very late, so he feels tired the next day.

2. Susan doesn't have enough free time to be with her boyfriend. She and her boyfriend both work at the hospital. The problem is, they both work different shifts at different times. This makes it hard for them to find time to be together.

3. Gary wants a promotion and a raise at work. Gary has worked at the same company for ten years. He likes his job but he feels he is ready for more responsibility.

4. Barbara wants to get better grades in school. She gets B's right now in most of her classes at high school. She would like to get A's.

5. Peter wants to learn how to drive. All his friends learned how to drive at driving school. Now, they all have their driver's license and he feels a little jealous.

6. Kathy wants more privacy at home. She lives with her parents and her younger brother and sister. She has to share a bedroom with her sister and she feels like she doesn't have enough privacy.

7. Michael wants to quit smoking. He is thirty-two years old and has smoked for fifteen years. He usually only smokes when he goes out with his friends and after he has dinner. He likes to have a cigarette at these times.

8. Jerry wants to lose weight. He is one hundred eighty centimeters tall. He weighs one hundred and ten kilograms. He would like to weigh ninety kilograms.

Who has which problem? Write their name next to their problem:

School grades -	Overweight -	Driving -	Smoking –
Schedule problems-	Work -	Privacy -	Insomnia -

Can you think of some advice for these people? How can they solve their problems? Write your suggestions and advice in the chart.

Person:	Advice:
John	
Susan	
Gary	
Barbara	
Peter	
Kathy	
Michael	
Jerry	

Discussion Questions:

1. How much sleep do you usually get each night?
2. Do you ever have trouble sleeping? What do you do about it?
3. Do you have enough free time?
4. How do you usually spend your free time?
5. What indoor activities do you like to do?
6. What outdoor activities do you like to do?
7. Did you ever get a promotion or a raise at work?
8. Would you like to have more or less responsibility in your life? Why?
9. How were your grades in school? Do you like to take tests? Why?
10. Which subjects were your favorites? Why?
11. Which subjects didn't you like? Why?

12. Do you know how to drive? How did you learn?
13. Do you like driving? Why?
14. Do you have enough privacy?
15. Did you ever have to share a bedroom?
16. Do you know anyone who smokes? How do you feel about smoking?
17. Why do people smoke? Why is it hard for smokers to quit?
18 How much do you weigh? How tall are you? Are you overweight, underweight, or are you just right?

Lesson 37 Emergencies: Robbery and Burglary

- What is the difference between robbery and burglary?
- What does a robber do? What does a burglar do?
- What should you do if someone tries to rob you?
- What would you do if you saw a bank robbery?
- How can you keep your home burglarproof?

Read about robberies and burglaries.

Robbers take things from people. They often carry a
weapon and threaten their victims. Robbers usually want
your wallet or purse. They want your cash and credit
cards. They also want your jewelry or watches. If a
robber tries to rob you, you shouldn't resist. You should
try to stay calm. If you resist the robber might hurt you,
since robbers often carry a weapon with them. You don't
want to get hurt, so you should give the robber what he or

she wants. Your life is more important than your money and jewelry. It is important to
try to remember what the robber looks like. You should report the robbery to the police
and they will ask for a physical description of the robber. You should report all crimes to
the police. It is their responsibility to help you, and it is your responsibility to cooperate
with and help them.

National crime statistics show that burglaries are increasing. This means that more and
more burglars are breaking into people's homes and stealing things. Almost one in five
homes has been a victim of burglary. That means twenty percent of homes have been
burglarized. Do not let your home and your family become victims of this crime. There
are some things that you can do to try to prevent burglaries and make your home safer
and more burglarproof. Here are some suggestions:

1. Install good, strong locks on all your house's doors. Make sure that all the doors are
   strong and cannot be broken into. Most burglars enter homes through doors.
2. Put metal bars over your windows. Burglars often enter through the windows.
3. Install a security system or a burglar alarm. These make noise when someone
   enters your home. Some security systems automatically call the police or a private
   security company.
4. Get to know your neighbors well. They can keep an eye on your home when you
   are away. You can do the same for them when they are away. Some
   neighborhoods have started 'neighborhood watch programs'. In these programs
   neighbors always keep an eye on each other's homes and are aware of anything that
   happens in their neighborhood.
5. If you are going on vacation stop delivery of the newspaper or any magazines.
   Second, ask a neighbor to pick up your mail everyday. Third, make sure your
   telephone has an answering machine. Ask callers to leave a message and tell them
   that you will call them back soon. This way, no one will know that you have gone
   away and your house should be safe from burglars and burglaries.

Comprehension Questions:

1. What do robbers do?
2. What do they usually carry?
3. What do they usually want?
4. What should you do if you are robbed?
5. How might you get hurt?
6. What is more important than your money and jewelry?
7. What should you report to the police?
8. What do national crime statistics show?
9. How many homes have been burglarized in the USA?
10. What should you install on your house's doors?
11. How do most burglars enter homes?
12. What should you put on your windows?
13. What should you install?
14. What do some security systems automatically do?
15. Who should you get to know well?
16. What can your neighbors do for you?
17. What should you do if you go away on vacation?
18. What should your telephone have?
19. Why do you need to do these things?

Discussion Questions:

1. If you were robbed, how would you feel? What would you do?
2. If a robber robbed you after class, what would he probably take from you?
3. If a robber robbed you, could you remember his appearance so you could describe him to the police?
4. How can you prevent being a robbery victim?
5. What is a good punishment for a robber?

6. Does your house have good, strong locks on all your house's doors? Are the doors strong?
7. Do you have metal bars over your windows?
8. Do you have a security system or a burglar alarm?
9. How well do you know your neighbors?
10. Do you have a newspaper delivered? Which one? How often is it delivered?
11. What other ways can you burglarproof your home?
12. How would you feel if your house was burgled?
13. If someone burgled your house, what things would they probably steal? What things would they not steal?
14. If someone wanted to burgle your house, how would they probably get in?

15. Which do you think is more serious: robbery or burglary? Why?
16. Which one is scarier to you: robbery or burglary? Why?
17. Would you rather be a robber or a burglar? Why?

Punishments

Parents punish children's bad behavior. Teachers punish student's bad behavior.
- Why do parents punish children? What kinds of behavior are punishable?
- Why do teachers punish students? What kinds of behavior are punishable?
- What kinds of punishment do parents give children?
- What kind of punishments do teachers give students?

Read about Tom and Jack.

Tom and Jack are junior high school students. They have known each other for a long time and are pretty good friends. They usually get along with each other very well. Today, however, the boys are not getting along so well. They have been arguing about Who is better: Superman or Spiderman. Tom thinks Superman is better than Spiderman. He thinks Superman is the strongest and fastest man on earth. He thinks no one is better than Superman. Jack thinks Spiderman is better than Superman. He thinks Spiderman is the bravest and smartest man on earth. He thinks no one is better than Spiderman. The boys started arguing on the school bus in the morning. Then, they continued their argument at lunch in the school cafeteria. Their argument became very strong and the boys started fighting. Tom smacked Jack in the mouth. Jack punched Tom in the stomach. Soon the two boys were rolling around on the floor of the cafeteria fighting. All the other students thought this was exciting and started to shout and cheer. "Come on Jack" some of them said. "Kill him Tom" some others said.

Before long, a teacher ran over to the boys and broke up the fight. Jack's mouth was bleeding and Tom's shirt was ripped. The teacher took Jack to the nurse's office and Tom to the principal's office. The nurse told Jack he would be okay and he went to the principal's office too. They both waited while the teacher explained to the principal what had happened. The principal asked the boys to tell him what had happened. They both gave their story and the principal listened. When they were finished the principal said that he understood the situation and that the boys would have to be punished. The principal thought for a minute about an appropriate punishment for the boys. Their punishment had four parts. First, the boys would have to stay after school for one week. They would help the janitor clean the school. Next, they would have to write one hundred times "I will not fight in school". Then, the principal made the boys shake hands and promise not to fight again. Finally, the principal told them he would have to call their parents to let them know what happened today in school.

The principal called their parents and explained the situation to them. Both boys' parents were surprised to hear that their sons were fighting because usually they got along so well. Tom and Jack's parents called each other after they had spoken to the principal. They both decided to ground the boys for two weeks. This means that for two weeks the boys could not leave the house after school and on the weekends. The boy's parents also decided to explain to their sons that Superman and Spiderman were both good, but in different ways.

Comprehension Questions:

1. Who are Tom and Jack?
2. How long have they been friends?
3. What is different today?
4. What are they arguing about?
5. What does Tom think?
6. What does Jack think?
7. When did they start fighting?
8. What did Tom do?
9. What did Jack do?
10. What did the other students think?
11. What did the other students say?
12. Who broke up the fight?
13. Where did the boys go?
14. What did the principal say?
15. What was their punishment?
16. Who did the principal call?
17. What was their parents' reaction?
18. What did their parents do?
19. How did their parents punish them?
19. What did their parents explain to them?

Discussion Questions:

1. Tom and Jack started fighting about Superman and Spiderman. What other things do kids fight about?
2. Did you ever get into a fight? What was it about? Who won the fight?
3. Kids also often argue. Who do they argue with? What do they argue about?
4. Do you think the punishments that Tom and Jack received were reasonable?
5. If you were the principal how would you have punished Tom and Jack?
6. If you were the parents how would you have punished Tom and Jack?
7. Was it fair for the boys to be punished at school and at home? Why?
8. How did your parents punish you when you were younger? Why did they punish you? Was your punishment fair or not?
9. How did your teachers punish you when you were a student? Why did they punish you? Was your punishment fair or not?
10. When someone breaks the law they are punished by the police or by a court. Think about the following crimes. What punishments do these crimes deserve? Write an appropriate punishment next to each crime:

- **Burglary (stealing jewelry and US $ 10,000)**
- **Speeding on the highway:**
- **Driving drunk:**
- **Murder:**
- **Arson:**
- **Smuggling weapons into the country:**
- **Fraud:**

Lesson 39   Television: Commercials

- Do you think TV commercials are entertaining?
- What do you usually do during TV commercials?
- Do you think TV has too many commercials?
- Do you have a favorite commercial? If so, what is it?
- What is the stupidest commercial you have ever seen?
- What is the funniest commercial you have ever seen?

Read about television commercials.

Television commercials have been around as long as the television itself. Companies found TV as an easier way to advertise their products to their customers. Today, companies spend millions of dollars promoting their products on TV. They advertise sodas, cars, computers, toys, beauty products, beer, cell phones, and anything you thought you would ever need. Most commercials usually last about 30 seconds. There are also commercials called infomercials. These can last anywhere from 30 minutes to an hour.

Many people think commercials are entertaining. During the Super bowl of American Football, advertisers spend millions of dollars for a 30 second commercial. Many people look forward to watching these commercials as much as the football game. They are often very creative and have celebrities in them. There are also people who do not like commercials. They find them too violent or too disruptive. Sometimes movies on television are cut so TV networks can show more commercials. Sporting events have timeouts so they can show more commercials.

There doesn't seem to be a solution to this problem. Television networks get paid by advertisers to show their commercials. If the TV program is popular, the networks usually charge more money and often show more commercials. So what should you do if you are annoyed by all the commercials? You can press the mute button on your remote control so you don't have to listen. You can change the channel and wait for your program to come back when the commercials are over. You can watch the commercials if you are interested in what they are selling. You can use the time to run to the bathroom, get something to eat or drink, or just turn off the TV and read a book.

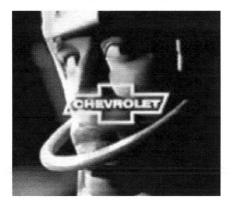

Comprehension Questions:

1. How long have TV commercials been around?
2. Why do companies advertise on TV?
3. What kinds of products are advertised on TV?
4. Is it expensive to advertise on TV?
5. How long are most commercials?
6. How long is an infomercial?
7. How much is a 30 second commercial during the Super bowl?
8. Why do some people like watching Super bowl commercials?
9. What are some reasons why some people dislike commercials?
10. Why do television networks sometimes cut movies?
11. Why do television networks show commercials?
12. When do networks charge more for commercials?
13. What can you do if you are annoyed by commercials?

Discussion Questions:

1. Do you generally like TV commercials? Why?
2. Do you think commercials can be entertaining or fun sometimes?
3. What TV commercials do you like? Why do you like them?
4. What commercials do you dislike? Why do you dislike them?
5. What's your favorite commercial? Why do you like it?
6. Do you like McDonald's commercials? Why?
7. Do you like commercials with celebrities in them? Who?
8. What kinds of commercials should not be on TV? Why not?

9. Do you ever buy things because you saw the commercial on TV? What?
10. Would you like to be in a TV commercial? What for?
11. Some commercials are funny. Give an example. Do you like this commercial?
12. Some commercials are serious. Give an example. Do you like this commercial?
13. Do you think people in commercials really like what they are advertising?
14. Do you like commercial breaks when you are watching a movie? Why?

15. What are some current commercials' slogans? What products are they for? Write them in the chart.

Slogan	Product

Lesson 40   Television Programs

- What is your favorite TV show? Why do you like it?
- What kind of show is it? Who are the stars?
- Do you watch it every week?
- What channel is it on? What day of the week is it on?
- What time does it begin? What time does it finish?

Read tonight's TV program listings.

8:00 PM

> **Channel 10**
> **CSI: Crime Scene Investigation (Drama)**
> In tonight's episode, the investigators try to track down the murderer of a 45 year old businessman found shot to death in his car.
>
> **Channel 45**
> **Friends (Comedy)**
> Chandler accidentally spills car oil all over Monica's favorite sweater and asks Joey and Ross to help clean it.
>
> **Channel 50**
> **Who Wants To Be A Millionaire (Game Show)**
> Watch our six new contestants answer questions. One lucky winner will win one million dollars by the end of the show.

9:00 PM

> **Channel 13**
> **Tomorrow Never Dies (Movie)**
> Pierce Brosnan stars as James Bond 007. This time Bond battles a media mogul who wants to start a war between China and England. Bond gets help from a Chinese spy played by Michelle Yeoh.
>
> **Channel 17**
> **English Premier League Football (Sports)**
> Tonight Liverpool takes on Manchester City in this long awaited game. Both teams have only two losses all year and are tied for first place.
>
> **Channel 23**
> **On The Road (Travel)**
> Your host Bill Lewis takes you on the road to Brazil. Join him as he explores the Amazon rainforest and walks the lively streets of Rio de Janeiro.
>
> **Channel 39**
> **Oprah Winfrey Show (Talk Show)**
> Oprah talks with singer/actress Madonna about her career and being a mother.

Comprehension Questions:

1. What kind of show is Friends?
2. What time is the travel show on tonight?
3. Who stars in the James Bond movie?
4. What channel is the Oprah Winfrey Show on?
5. What is tonight's episode of CSI about?
6. What teams are playing in the English Premier match?
7. Which team is better?
8. What channel is Friends on?
9. Who is the host of the travel show?
10. What is the name of the game show?
11. How much does the winner receive on the game show?
12. What is Tomorrow Never dies about?
13. What channel is the football game on?
14. What kind of show is CSI?
15. What is the travel show's destination?
16. What time is Oprah on tonight?
17. Who is the guest on the Oprah Winfrey Show?
18. What is tonight's episode of Friends about?
19. What time is the James Bond movie on?
20. What time is Friends on?

Discussion Questions:

1. What kind of television shows do you usually watch?
2. When do you usually watch TV?
3. Do you think TV is educational?
4. How often do you watch TV?
5. How much is too much TV?
6. Do you think there is too much violence on TV?
7. What are some of the advantages of watching TV?
8. What are some of the disadvantages of watching TV?
9. Did you watch TV yesterday? What did you watch?
10. Do you like to watch talk shows?

11. Who is your favorite talk show host? Why?
12. Do you like game shows?
13. Do you ever watch educational TV?
14. Do you think educational TV is entertaining? Why?
15. Do you think watching TV makes you lazy?
16. What can people learn from watching TV?
17. Would you rather read a novel or watch TV? Why?
18. How can TV be useful for children? What can children learn from TV?
19. How can TV be a bad influence for children? What negative effects can TV have?
20. How many TV sets do you have in your house? Where are they?

Lesson 41   Transportation Schedules

- Have you ever traveled by train? Where?
- What can passengers do on a train?
- Is the train service in your country reliable?
- Have you ever traveled by airplane? Where?
- What can passengers do on an airplane?
- Do you think flying is exciting or boring? Why?
- Why are some people afraid to fly? Are you?

- Can you read a transportation schedule? Let's find out...

Train Schedule: Eurostar.

Eurostar is a popular European train service. Eurostar is a train service that connects London with Lille, Paris, and Brussels. Trains cross the English Channel through the Channel tunnel. The French and Belgian parts of the line are high-speed rail, and since September 2003, so is part of the route in England, the Channel Tunnel Rail Link.

London to Paris takes 2 hours 35 minutes. London to Brussels takes 2 hours and 20 minutes. The company that runs Eurostar is a joint venture between Belgian, French and British railway companies. British Pounds and Euros may be used to buy refreshments on the trains. The border between France and the UK is in the middle of the tunnel.

DEPART LONDON	EUROSTAR TRAIN NO	ARRIVE BRUSSELS	NOTES
614	9108	1002	Mon-Sat
653	9110	1037	Mon-Fri
827	9116	1210	
1027	9124	1405	
1227	9132	1610	
1423	9140	1802	
1627	9148	2010	
1719	9152	2106	Departs 1723 Sat, 1727 Sun
1827	9156	2210	Except Sat
1927	9160	2310	

Questions:

1. What is Eurostar?
2. Which cities does Eurostar connect?
3. How do trains cross the English Channel?
4. How long does London to Paris take?
5. How long does London to Brussels take?
6. Which currencies can passengers use on the train?

7. Where is the British and French border?
8. What time does train 9108 depart London?
9. What time does train 9116 arrive in Brussels?
10. Does train 9148 arrive in Brussels at 2110?
11. Does train 9108 run on Sundays?
12. Does train 9156 run on Saturdays?
13. What time does train 9152 depart on Sundays?
14. Which train arrives in Brussels at 2010?
15. Which train departs London at 1227?

Airline Schedule: These flights leave Taipei and arrive in San Francisco.

Depart TPE	Arrive SFO	Airline	Stop	Trip Time
7:00 a.m.	8:45 a.m.	China Airlines	Hong Kong	17:45
8:40 a.m.	8:35 a.m.	Eva	Osaka	15:55
9:15 a.m.	7:30 a.m.	Northwest	Tokyo	14:15
10:30 a.m.	10:00 a.m.	United	Tokyo	15:30
4:35 p.m.	5:30 p.m.	Cathay Pacific	Hong Kong	16:55
8:20 p.m.	7:35 p.m.	Japan Airlines	Hong Kong	15:15
10:55 p.m.	1130 p.m.	Singapore Air	Los Angeles	16:35

Questions:

1. How many flights are there?
2. Which is the earliest flight? Which is the latest?
3. What time does China Airlines depart Taipei?
4. What time does Eva Airlines arrive in San Francisco?
5. If you want to leave Taipei in the afternoon, which flight would you take?
6. If you want a night flight, which flight would you take?
7. Which airline has the longest trip time? The shortest?
8. Are there any direct flights?
9. Where does Singapore Air stop?
10. Where does United Airlines stop?
11. How many flights stop in Hong Kong?
12. If you had to choose from these flights, which one would you pick? Why?

Discussion Questions:

1. Do you prefer to travel by train or by airplane? Why?
2. What is the longest train journey you have ever taken? How long was it?
3. What is the longest flight you have ever taken? How long was it?
4. Would you like to travel in Europe? Where would you like to go?
5. Would you like to travel in the USA? Where would you like to go?
6. What do you know about San Francisco?
7. What do you know about Tokyo?
8. What do you know about London?
9. What do you know about Brussels?

Lesson 42   Transportation

- How do you usually get around?
- What is your favorite way to travel?
- Would you rather take a train or a plane? Why?
- Which is more comfortable: an airplane or a train?
- Do you ever get carsick? Airsick? Seasick?
- Have you ever been on a boat? Where?
- Would you like to go on a cruise? Why?
- Can you swim well? Are you a good swimmer?
- What causes air pollution?

Read about some different kinds of transportation.

There are many different kinds of transportation. People use different kinds of transportation for different reasons. For short journeys people often use small, personal transportation such as a bicycle or scooter. People also ride a bicycle for exercise. For longer journeys people might drive their car or truck. Some people prefer to ride a motorcycle. People often use their personal transportation to get to work, to go shopping, or to run errands. People also take a ride or a drive on the weekends.

There are different kinds of public transportation as well as personal transportation.
Many people take a bus or subway to school or to work in the mornings. Some people take a taxi to get to where they want to go. Some cities have trams or cable cars for passengers to take. Electric trams are a good way to save energy and reduce the amount of pollution in large cities. Too much traffic and transportation cause a lot of air and noise pollution. Some cities have car pool programs to reduce the amount of traffic and pollution in their city. Car pools are people who travel together in one car.

Some people have jobs that require them to use special kinds of transportation. A chauffeur drives wealthy people around in a limousine. A pilot flies an airplane or perhaps even a helicopter. Factory workers might need to operate a forklift. Truck drivers drive large trucks to transport goods to places far away. Astronauts need to know how to fly and to control a spaceship. Racecar drivers need to know how to drive very fast. Many people think that this is an exciting but dangerous job.

People use different kinds of transportation when they travel or go on vacation. For long journeys travelers often take an airplane. Some flights are short, others are very long. It depends on where you want to go. Some travelers like to go on a cruise. This is a journey on a very luxurious ship. The ship has many facilities and recreational activities for passengers to take part in. The cruise ship sails on the ocean and stops at various ports along the way. Passengers can debark the ship and explore different kinds of local cultures and lifestyles. Then, they can buy souvenirs to take home.

* What other kinds of transportation can you think of? Make a list. *

Comprehension Questions:

1. There are many different kinds of what?
2. What do people often use for short journeys?
3. What do people often use for longer journeys?
4. What do people use their personal transportation for?
5. What do people also do on the weekends?
6. What kind of transportation is there besides personal?
7. How do some people get to work or to school?
8. What do some cities have?
9. How are electric trams beneficial?
10. What can too much traffic and transportation cause?
11. What do some cities have? What is this?
12. What does a chauffeur do?
13. What do pilots fly?
14. What do racecar drivers need to know how to do?
15. What do many people think about this job?
16. When do people use different kinds of transportation?
17. What does the length of the flight depend on?
18. What is a cruise?
19. What can passengers do on a cruise?
20. Where do cruise ships stop?
21. What can passengers buy?

Discussion Questions:

1. Do you own a car? What color is it? Why did you buy this kind?
2. Do you have a driver's license? When did you get your license?
3. Do you always wear your seatbelt when you ride in a car? Why?
4. Should people be allowed to talk on the telephone while they drive? Why?
5. Do you think car pools are a good idea? Why?
6. Have you ever taken a taxi? When? Where did you go?
7. If you were going to buy a car which kind would you buy?
8. Is parking a problem in your city? What are the problems?
9. What kinds of public transportation can people use in your country?
10. How often do you use public transportation?

11. What kind of transportation do you use most often? Why?
12. What do you think is the most reliable form of transportation? Why?
13. When was the last time you went on a train? Where did you go? Why did you go?
14. Do you ever ride a bicycle? How often? Where do you go?
15. Would you like to be a truck driver? Why?
16. How many times have you flown on an airplane? Where did you go?
17. Have you ever been abroad? Where did you go?
18. Where would you like to go?
19. Would you like to go on a cruise? Where would you like to go?
20. Do you ever get travel sickness (carsick, seasick, or airsick)?
21. What should you do if you get travel sickness?

Lesson 43   San Francisco, London, Hong Kong

- Where is San Francisco? What do you know about it?
- Where is London? What do you know about it?
- Where is Hong Kong? What do you know about it?

Read about what you can see and do in each of the three cities.

San Francisco:

- Go hiking in the forest.
- Go to the San Francisco Zoo.
- Visit shops and seafood restaurants at Fisherman's Wharf.
- Ride on a cable car.
- See the Golden Gate Bridge.
- See the San Francisco Giants play baseball at Pacific Bell Park.
- See the giant redwood trees in Muir Woods forest.

London:

- Ride in the London Eye.
- Visit the British Museum.
- See Buckingham Palace.
- See Big Ben and the Houses of Parliament.
- Go to traditional English pubs.
- Take a walk by the Thames River.
- See the London Symphony.

Hong Kong:

- Take a tram to Victoria Peak to see the fantastic view of Hong Kong.
- Go from Kowloon to Hong Kong Island on the Star Ferry.
- Eat Cantonese dim sum and fresh seafood.
- Go shopping at Stanley Market.
- Take a helicopter tour of Hong Kong.
- Watch horse racing at Happy Valley racetrack.
- Play golf on LanTau Island.

85

Comprehension Questions:

1. Where can you go hiking in San Francisco?
2. Where can you go shopping there?
3. What special transportation can you take?
4. Which famous bridge can you see?
5. Which baseball team can you see?
6. What special trees can you see?

7. Which museum can you visit in London?
8. Where can you maybe see the queen?
9. Which famous clock can you see?
10. Where can you get a pint of English beer?
11. Where can you take a walk in London?
12. What kind of music can you hear?

13. What can you see from Victoria Peak?
14. Where can you go on the Star Ferry?
15. What local food can you eat in Hong Kong?
16. Where can you go shopping in Hong Kong?
17. Where can you gamble?
18. Where can you play golf?

Discussion questions:

1. Have you ever been to San Francisco? Would you like to go?
2. Have you ever been to London? Would you like to go?
3. Have you ever been to Hong Kong? Would you like to go?

4. Which one of the three destinations sounds best for a vacation? Why?
5. Which of the activities above do you think is most interesting? Why?
6. Which of the activities above do you think is most uninteresting? Why?
7. Would you prefer to go to a city or the countryside for a vacation? Why?

8. Where have you been on vacation? What did you do there?
9. What do you like to do when you are on vacation?
10. Do you like to go shopping on vacation? Where do you like to go shopping?
11. What kinds of things do you like to buy?

12. If you could go anywhere in the world on vacation where would you go? What would you do there? Who would you go with?
13. Would you rather take a vacation in Asia or in Europe? Why?
14. Would you rather take a vacation in America or in England? Why?
15. How is London different from San Francisco?
16. How is London different from Hong Kong?
17. How is London similar to Hong Kong?

Lesson 44   Bali Island and Nepal

- Where is Nepal? What do you know about it?
- Would you like to visit there? Why?
- Where is Bali Island? What do you know about it?
- Would you like to visit there? Why?
- What can visitors and tourists do in these places?

Read about Bali Island and Nepal.

Bali is a beautiful island in Indonesia. There are many things for tourists to do on Bali Island. You can play and relax on the beach. You can go swimming, snorkeling, or scuba diving. You can eat fresh seafood. You can visit Bali's Hindu temples. If you want to go shopping you can buy souvenirs and local handcrafts in the traditional market. Bali is a great vacation destination, and it is generally reasonably priced.

Nepal is in the Himalayan Mountains. It is a land of beautiful scenery, ancient temples, and some of the best walking trails on earth. It's a poor country, but it is very scenic and has many cultural treasures. This is why so many travelers are attracted to Nepal. In Nepal most tourists go hiking in the mountains. There are many different routes and trails to go on. Some are day hikes, some are three-week hikes. You can go for as long as you like. It just depends on how long you want to go. All tourists need visas to enter Nepal. Single-entry visas cost US$30.

There are some health risks in Nepal. These include altitude sickness, hepatitis A, and malaria. Altitude sickness comes from being at a high altitude. Hepatitis can come from food. Malaria is carried by mosquitoes. When you travel, you have to try to stay healthy. It is important to eat carefully and try not to get sick. Many people get food poisoning from eating badly prepared or spoiled food. Also, it is important to try to get regular exercise to keep your body strong and healthy.

Comprehension Questions:

1. Where is Bali Island?
2. What can tourists do there?
3. What can tourists eat on Bali?
4. What kind of temples can you visit in Bali?
5. What kinds of things can you buy in Bali?
6. Is a Bali vacation expensive?
7. Where is Nepal?
8. Is Nepal a rich country?
9. Why are travelers attracted to Nepal?
10. Where can you go hiking?
11. How long are the hikes?
12. Who needs a visa for Nepal?
13. How much does a visa cost?
14. How can you get altitude sickness?
15. How can you get malaria?
16. How can you get food poisoning?

Discussion Questions:

1. Have you ever been to Nepal? Would you like to go? Why?
2. Have you ever been to Bali Island? Would you like to go? Why?
3. Have you ever been to a beautiful beach? Where? What did you see and do?
4. Have you ever been to some beautiful mountains? Where?
5. Would you rather go to Bali Island or to Nepal? Why?
6. Do you like to travel? Why?
7. Where would you like to travel? Why do you want to go there?
8. Where would you not want to travel? Why not?
9. Do you prefer to relax on vacation or do you prefer an active vacation? Why?

10. Would you rather travel in Asia or Europe? Why?
11. What things do you need to take with you on vacation?
12. What would you need to take for a beach vacation?
13. What would you need to take for a mountain vacation?
14. Would you prefer to have a beach vacation or a mountain vacation? Why?
15. What would you do on a beach vacation?
16. What would you do on a mountain vacation?
17. Where is a good destination for a beach vacation?
18. Where is a good destination for a mountain vacation?

- **Which would you take to the beach? Which would you take to the mountains? Which would you take to both the beach and the mountains?**

Sunscreen	Sunglasses	Sweater	Backpack	Sandals	Hiking boots	Sun hat
Map	Hammock	Guide book	Camera	Extra clothes	Swimsuit	Sarong
Cooler	Water bottle	Walking stick	Binoculars	Frisbee	Flashlight	Towel
Guide book	Money	Notebook and pencil	Cell phone	Umbrella		

- **Write your answers in this chart.**

Take to the beach	Take to the mountains	Take to both

- What are some good points of living in the city?
- What are some bad points of living in the city?
- What are some good points of living in the countryside?
- What are some bad points of living in the countryside?
- Do you live in the city, the suburbs, or the countryside?
- Do you like where you live? Why?
- Where else have you lived?
- Which place that you have lived did you like best? Why?

Read about some positive and negative sides to urban life.

There are many positive sides to urban life. Living in a city can be very convenient. There are many places to go shopping where people can buy things that they need. Many of these places are open until late at night. So, you can buy almost anything you want very easily at almost any time of day. There is usually a lot of variety in a city. There are many different choices of things to do and places to go. There are different choices for entertainment and recreation. People can go to see a movie or a show. They can go shopping or enjoy a walk in a park. They can visit museums and art galleries. They can go to a zoo or to sporting event. Cities also usually have a wide selection of restaurants, cafes, and places to eat. You can usually find many different kinds of restaurants in a big city. These restaurants usually offer a good selection of international cuisine and local food. People who live in a city also have many educational options and opportunities. They can go to different schools to learn different things, depending on their interests. An urban environment also provides a wide variety of employment opportunities. There are many different kinds of jobs in many different fields and professions. A city is usually very convenient in terms of transportation. People can take a bus, a train, a subway, a taxi, or other kinds of transportation. There is usually an airport near a city so it can be convenient for flying as well. Some cities are located near water, so this makes travel by water possible too. Generally, urban life is convenient and offers people who live there a lot of variety and different opportunities.

However, there are many negative sides to urban life. Urban environments are generally crowded because many people live in a small area. This also affects the traffic situation. Cities often have traffic jams that can delay a person's plans and make them a little frustrated. Sometimes workers need to repair the roads in a city. This also can cause traffic delays and hold-ups. These kinds of things can be annoying for people who live in a city. Other problems associated with urban life are litter and pollution. Sometimes urban environments can be dirty. This is because some people are not responsible with their trash, and throw it on the ground. This causes litter on the streets. Air pollution is caused by the traffic in the city. Cars, motorcycles, trucks, and buses are constantly polluting the air with their exhaust fumes. Another source of pollution is factories. Factories produce industrial pollution. Some other problems associated with urban life are crime and a high cost of living.

Comprehension Questions:

1. What is one positive side to urban life?
2. Where can people buy what they need?
3. How late are these places open?
4. What kind of variety is there in a city?
5. What can people visit in a city?
6. What kinds of restaurants are in a city?
7. What other options and opportunities do people who live in a city have?
8. What transportation options do they have?
9. What is a negative side of urban life?
10. Why are urban areas generally crowded?
11. What does this affect?
12. What else can cause traffic delays?
13. What other problems are associated with urban life?
14. What causes air pollution?
15. What are some other problems associated with urban life?

Discussion Questions:

1. Why do so many people want to live in cities?
2. What would an optimistic city-dweller say about shopping?
3. What would a pessimistic city-dweller say?
4. What would an optimistic city-dweller say about traffic?
5. What would a pessimistic city-dweller say?
6. What would an optimistic city-dweller say about schools?
7. What would a pessimistic city-dweller say?
8. What would an optimistic city-dweller say about the police?
9. What would a pessimistic city-dweller say?
10. What would an optimistic city-dweller say about parks?
11. What would a pessimistic city-dweller say?

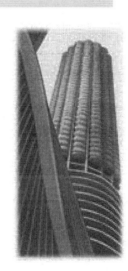

12. Which is the biggest city you have ever been to? Did you like it? What did you do there?
13. What other cities have you been to? Did you like them?
14. Do you live in a city? Why?
15. Do you like where you live? Why?
16. Where else have you lived? Which place did you like best? Why?
17. Which is better: to live in a city or to live in the countryside? Why?

18. What do you know about these cities: New York, Los Angeles, Tokyo, Bangkok, Paris, London, Toronto, Hong Kong, and Singapore?

19. Which of these cities would you like to visit? Why?
20. Which of these cities would not you like to visit? Why?

Look at these different vehicles. Say something about each one.

Questions:

1. What kinds of people drive convertibles?
2. What kind of weather do you need to appreciate a convertible?
3. What kind of weather is not good for a convertible?
4. Which of these vehicles are appropriate for a family to use?
5. What are the advantages of having a hatchback?
6. What are the drawbacks to having a hatchback?
7. What are the advantages of having a jeep?
8. What are the drawbacks to having a jeep?
9. What kinds of people drive sports cars?

10. Name some different kinds of sports cars.
11. What are the advantages of having a pickup truck?
12. What are the drawbacks of having a pickup truck?
13. What are the advantages of having a recreational vehicle?
14. What are the drawbacks of having a recreational vehicle?
15. If you had a recreational vehicle where would you go?
16. Why do some people like to drive vans?
17. Say something good about big trucks.
18. Say something bad about big trucks.

Look at these road signs. What do they mean?

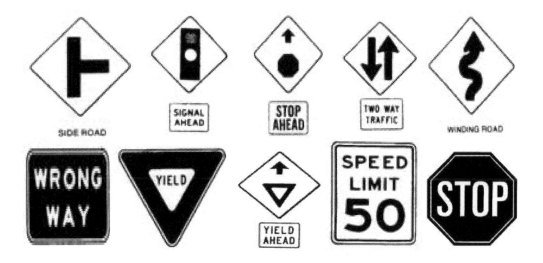

SIDE ROAD

SIGNAL AHEAD

STOP AHEAD

TWO WAY TRAFFIC

WINDING ROAD

WRONG WAY

YIELD

YIELD AHEAD

SPEED LIMIT 50

STOP

Discussion Questions:

1. What should you do when you see a red light?
2. What should you do when you see a green light?
3. What should you do when you see a yellow light?
4. What should you do when it's raining?
5. What should you do when it's foggy?

6. Can you drive a car? Are you a good driver?
7. Are you a fast driver? Are you a safe driver?
8. What kind of car do you or your family have?
9. What is the speed limit where you live?
10. What is the speed limit on the highway?
11. Do you ever drive over the speed limit?
12. Why do people drive over the speed limit?

13. What can cause traffic accidents?
14. What should you do if you see a traffic accident?
15. What should you do if you have a traffic accident?
16. How can you prevent traffic accidents?
17. Two cars approach an intersection at the same time. One is driving east and the other is driving north. Which one has the right of way? Which one should yield?

18. There is a red line next to the sidewalk. What does this mean?
19. There is a broken line in the middle of the road. What does this mean?
20. There is a double-yellow line in the middle of the road. What does this mean?

Lesson 47   Outdoor Activities

- Do you prefer to spend time outside or inside?
- What indoor activities do you enjoy?
- What outdoor activities do you enjoy?
- What do you like to do on your day off?
- Have you ever been camping? Where did you go?
- Why do some people enjoy camping?
- Have you ever stayed in a nice hotel? Where?

Read about Dan and Lydia's camping trip.

Dan and Lydia are going camping this weekend. Dan loves the outdoors but Lydia would rather go to the big city and stay in a fancy hotel. Lydia agreed to go camping this weekend if Dan promised that they could go to Taipei next weekend.

Dan has packed up the car with everything they will need. He has a tent, sleeping bags, lantern, grill, and a cooler. They are going to Yu Shan National Park and will leave early Saturday morning. Dan wants to get an early start so they can miss all the traffic. First, they will find a campsite and set up camp. Then, they will go to the local store to buy some food and drinks. In the afternoon, they will go hiking. Dan loves to go bird watching. Lydia just bought him a new pair of binoculars and Dan is excited to try them. He is looking forward to seeing the natural beauty of the countryside.

After the hike, they will go for a swim in the river. The water isn't too deep so swimming in the river is safe. Then, they will have a picnic in the woods. The views are beautiful from the top of the mountain. You can see waterfalls, trees, flowers, and wild animals.

Dan is going to grill hotdogs and hamburgers for dinner. He'll build a campfire before sunset to keep them warm during the night. They'll roast marshmallows for dessert and sit around the campfire admiring the night sky. On Sunday, they will wake up early, take a small hike, and then go to the hot springs. Lydia likes the hot springs because the water is good for your skin and you can relax in the soothing water.

After they return from the hot springs, they'll take down the tent, clean up their campsite, and drive home. A weekend in the mountains can leave you feeling relaxed and refreshed. Going on a camping trip is a good way to get a break from the city.

Comprehension Questions:

1. Where are Dan and Lydia going this weekend?
2. Who loves the outdoors?
3. What would Lydia rather do?
4. What has Dan packed in the car?
5. When will Dan and Lydia leave?
6. Why does Dan want to get an early start?
7. What will they do after they set up camp?
8. Where will they have a picnic?
9. What is Dan excited to try out?
10. What is he looking forward to?
11. What will Dan make for dinner?
12. What will they have for dessert?
13. Why will they have a campfire?
14. Where will they go after the hike on Sunday morning?
15. Why does Lydia like the hot springs?
16. What will they do when they return from the hot springs?
17. How can a weekend in the mountains make you feel?
18. What is a good way to get a break from the city?

Discussion Questions:

1. Do you like camping? Why or why not?
2. If you went to the mountains, what would you do?
3. Have you ever been fishing? Is fishing a relaxing thing to do? How?

4. Why do some people hunt animals? How do you feel about this?
5. What are some things that people usually bring when they go hiking?
6. Is it important to bring a garbage bag when you go hiking or camping? Why?
7. What animals have you seen in the mountains?
8. What should you do for a bee sting? Snake bite? Rash?

9. Some people tell ghost stories around campfires. Do you like scary stories?
10. If you went camping overnight, what kind of food would you bring?

11. Is pollution a serious problem in your country?
12. What are the major sources of pollution?
13. What different kinds of pollution are there?
14. How can people help to reduce different kinds of pollution?

15. Are you a wasteful person? What do you waste? How can you reduce waste?
16. How can we make our community cleaner?
17. Are you worried about these kinds of things or not? Why?

Lesson 48 Vacations: Camping and Package Tours

- Why do some people enjoy camping?
- Have you ever been camping? Where did you go? How was it?
- Where are some popular camping spots?
- Why do some people like to travel with a package tour?
- Have you ever been on a package tour? Where did you go? How was it?

Harry likes to go camping on vacation.

Harry: I enjoy going camping with my family on vacation. Sometimes we like to go to the mountains and find a good camping spot. This is good because it is quiet and isolated. We can enjoy the peaceful natural scenery and breathe the fresh mountain air. There are many things to do when we go camping. First, we have to find a good flat spot. Then, we have to unpack all our camping equipment and supplies and put up the tent. We have to take a lot of things with us when we go camping. We take camping equipment and supplies. After we have set up the tent, we usually take a walk around the camping spot to find some dry wood for a campfire. It's great to be surrounded by nature. The mountains are beautiful. There are many trees and sometimes there is a river or stream. Sometimes we camp next to a lake. The kids can go swimming and I can relax as I try to catch some fish.

Julie likes to travel with package tours.

Julie: I like to travel with a package tour. Package tours are very convenient. Everything is arranged and organized for you. The schedule is made and you don't have to make any big decisions. Package tours are perfect for me. I pay my money and the tour organizers take care of everything. When I go on vacation I don't want to have to think about where to stay, what to do, or where to eat. All of these things are taken care of by the tour group company, so I can relax. I do not have to worry about anything. Last year, my friend and I went on a package tour to the Bahamas. We stayed in a great hotel by the beach. Everything was arranged for us and we had a great time. The tour and the hotel had organized lots of different activities for the guests to join. Sometimes we joined the activities and sometimes we did our own things. The hotel also had scooters available to ride around the island for sightseeing, so we also were able to be independent and make our own schedule if we wanted. This year, we are thinking about going to Greece. Of course, we'll choose to join a package tour. They're so much fun and very convenient.

Comprehension Questions:

1. Where do Harry and his family enjoy camping?
2. Why do they like it there?
3. How is the scenery? How is the air?
4. What do they have to do first?
5. What do they have to unpack?
6. What do they have to put up?
6. What do they do after they have put up the tent?
7. What kind of nature can they see?
8. What can the kids do if they camp near a lake?
9. What can Harry do at the lake?

11. Why does Julie like package tours?
12. What doesn't Julie want to have to do on vacation?
13. Where did Julie and her friend go last year?
14. Where did they stay?
15. What was arranged for them?
16. What did the hotel and tour group organize?
17. Did they join all the activities?
18. What did they sometimes do?
19. How did they get around the island?
20. Where will they go next year?

Discussion Questions:

1. Make a list of ten things you would need to take for a three-day camping trip to the mountains. Does this kind of trip sound interesting to you? Why?
2. Name some good camping areas that you know about. Which would you like to visit?

3. Harry likes to go camping. He mentioned many positive points about going camping. Of course there are negative points as well. How many can you think of?

4. Julie likes to join package tours. She mentioned many positive points about package tours. Of course there are negative points as well. How many can you think of?

5. Would you like to go on a package tour? Where would you like to go? Why would you like to go there? What kinds of things will you do there?
6. What things are usually in a hotel room? Make a list of ten things.

7. Which looks more comfortable; the tent or the hotel? Why?
8. Which is more interesting to you: camping or a package tour? Why?

9. Where have you traveled? What did you do there? Did you have a good time?
10. Where would you like to travel? What would you like to do and see there?
11. What places would you recommend to tourists visiting your country?
12. Have you ever been to these places? What did you do there?
13. If you had two weeks off, would you rather go camping, join a package tour, or stay at home and relax?   Why?

Made in the USA
Middletown, DE
28 July 2018